Teaching
Conflict Resolution
Through
Children's Literature

by William J. Kreidler

SCHOLASTIC
PROFESSIONAL BOOKS

NEW YORK • TORONTO • LONDON • AUCKLAND • SYDNEY

For G. Frederic Evans
In Memoriam

ACKNOWLEDGMENTS

There are many people who helped make this book a reality. I'd like to thank my colleagues at Boston Area Educators for Social Responsibility. From the beginning, Rachel Poliner encouraged me to go ahead with our children's literature work even when others didn't understand why we were doing it. Sally Orme shared her extensive experience as a teacher, mother, and children's book expert. Carol Wintle asked the questions that got me to explain the approach and the activities clearly. I'd also like to thank David Aronstein for his support and patience.

At Scholastic, Terry Cooper called me up and asked me to write a book on conflict resolution. I thank her for her enthusiasm for this project, her insightful criticism, and her willingness to drop everything to talk. Finally, I'd like to thank the thousands of teachers and students over the years who suggested books and gave me feedback on the activities. Here's the book you asked for.

Interior design by Jacqueline Swensen
Cover and interior illustrations by James Graham Hale
Cover design by Vincent Ceci

ISBN 0-590-49747-2

12 11 10 9 8 7 6 5 4 3 2 1   4/5

Printed in the U.S.A.

Table of Contents

Introduction

Recently two second graders presented me with a picture they had just completed. "We're finally finished," said one. "Some crayons broke, just like in *Matthew and Tilly*, but we only went part way up the Conflict Escalator. Then we worked it out."

"Yeah," said her partner. "We made a thumbs-up agreement."

"That's great," I said. "How did you do it?"

"Mr. Kreidler," the first child said solemnly, "It takes a lot of trust."

When I told that story in a workshop for teachers, one of the participants said, "I would love it if my kids had those kinds of skills. But where do I find the time to teach them?"

Teaching Conflict Resolution Through Children's Literature is the book for that teacher and for any teacher who would like to help primary grade students become more effective and independent in handling conflicts. Its purpose is to help you teach conflict resolution and other social skills as you work with children on reading and language arts.

In many ways, children's literature is an ideal vehicle for teaching conflict resolution and other social skills. Children's literature can be used to:

* *introduce, model, and reinforce conflict resolution skills;*

* *develop understanding and concepts about conflict;*

* *develop core themes and values in the classroom.*

HOW TO USE THIS BOOK

Teaching Conflict Resolution Through Children's Literature is divided into eight chapters, each based on a conflict or conflict resolution concept. Each chapter features:

* *an introduction to the conflict resolution concept;*

* *introductory activities and extension activities;*

* *books to reinforce and extend the concept, including suggestions for introducing books, discussion questions, and follow-up activities;*

* *additional books and activities that build on the themes of the chapter.*

To begin using the book, introduce the conflict resolution activities in Chapter One, "What Is Conflict?" Then follow up with one or two of the suggested books and activities to reinforce the conflict resolution concepts and skills. When you feel children have a good understanding of the chapter's content, move on to Chapter Two, "The Conflict Escalator." You do not need to use all of the books or activities suggested in a chapter before you move on. In fact, it's a good idea to revisit the concept using a new book after children have worked with other conflict resolution skills.

My own experience and the experience of other teachers shows that this pattern of introducing the conflict resolution concept and following it up with reading and literature-based activities works best. Almost every other aspect of *Teaching Conflict Resolution Through Children's Literature* is flexible. You know your students and their needs, and you should trust your instincts to discover what will be most useful and enjoyable for them.

Experiment! For example, the recommended books may be read aloud to the whole class or used with small reading groups. The discussion questions are only suggestions. I hope they will lead your class into a dynamic and fruitful dialogue, but feel free to add your own and build on what the class is contributing. You will also find that the activities are very adaptable. You may decide that an activity for a mural may work better as a bulletin board, or an activity sheet based on writing may work better as a springboard for discussion. For students who are non-readers and writers, most of the activities can be adapted to meet their skill levels.

The Peaceable Classroom Model*

Teaching Conflict Resolution Through Children's Literature is based on an approach called the Peaceable Classroom Model. The Peaceable Classroom approach looks at the classroom as a caring and respectful community. Five themes are emphasized:

- ✦ *cooperation*
- ✦ *communication*
- ✦ *emotional expression*
- ✦ *appreciation for diversity*
- ✦ *conflict resolution*

You will see these five themes throughout this book. Some are the focus of individual chapters, but all of them are infused into every aspect of the book. Obviously, conflict resolution is the main theme of the book. But you will find that most of the activities are cooperatively structured and encourage children to communicate with each other. Similarly, the activities encourage children to identify and discuss the affective aspects of the books used. Many of the books model cultural and ethnic diversity as well as other types of diversity.

The reason for this emphasis on the themes of the Peaceable Classroom is simple. Conflict resolution is most effectively taught not in isolation, but in the context of this caring and respectful community. Establishing a Peaceable Classroom is one of the ways you can prevent conflict by addressing some of the root causes of classroom conflict. Belonging to a caring classroom community can motivate children to resolve conflict nonviolently. The Peaceable Class-

*The Peaceable Classroom model is discussed more thoroughly in my previous books, *Creative Conflict Resolution* (Scott Foresman and Co., 1984) and *Elementary Perspectives: Teaching Concepts of Peace and Conflict* (Educators for Social Responsibility, 1991.)

room approach is also an important part of creating a total conflict resolution program in a classroom or school.

A Total Conflict Resolution Program

Teaching Conflict Resolution Through Children's Literature is designed to help you develop a total conflict resolution program in your elementary classroom. The program has three elements:

+ **teaching the skills and concepts children need to resolve conflict nonviolently;**

+ **infusing the principles of conflict resolution into the standard curriculum;**

+ **modeling conflict resolution and creating a classroom environment that supports conflict resolution and prosocial behavior.**

This book deals primarily with teaching skills and concepts, and infusing these skills and concepts into the standard curriculum. The third element is partly addressed by implementing a Peaceable Classroom approach. But there's another aspect too. We, as classroom teachers, need to take an honest look at how we handle conflicts—those that occur between children, and those that occur between children and ourselves. Are we setting a good example? What are children learning as they watch us handle conflicts? What conflict resolution skills do we need to learn or practice?

I don't mean to imply that we should negotiate every conflict that comes up in our classrooms. But there should be a general consistency between what we do and what we ask children to do. If we want children to listen to each other, we need to model that skill. If we want them to be respectful, we need to treat them with respect.

A Three-Minute Introduction to Conflict Resolution

Since all of us can improve in the ways we handle conflict, the following quick introduction focuses on some of the key concepts that underlie the activities in this book.

Conflicts are a normal and natural part of everyone's life. Conflicts are simply the disputes and disagreements that occur between people. While we tend to think of conflict only in terms of its negative effects, the fact is that conflict can also be very positive. Without conflict, there is no growth or progress. There is stagnation. It is the constructive use of conflict that allows society to move forward.

The goal of conflict resolution education is not to eliminate conflict. That is impossible. Instead, its aim is to help children learn from conflict and use it for its constructive potential. By doing so, they can avoid the destructive aspects of conflict.

Many children—and adults—look at conflict as a contest in which one person wins and the other loses. This book promotes *win-win* conflict resolution, where all parties get what they need and feel good about the resolution.

Conflict resolution is an umbrella term that covers everything from a punch in the nose to sitting down and talking. There is no one right way to handle all conflicts. Different conflict resolution approaches are appropriate for different situations. The activities in this book will help children recognize options in conflict situations, and will encourage them to choose options that are nonviolent, meet the needs of the people involved, and improve relationships.

Developmental Considerations in Teaching Conflict Resolution*

There are developmental considerations to keep in mind as you work with primary grade children. Developmental concerns will be explained in the appropriate chapters, but here are some general guidelines.

+ *Think in terms of readiness as well as mastery. Many conflict resolution skills and concepts such as problem solving and point of view, are difficult for young children. Children may not be ready to master the skill or concept. They are able to work at a readiness level, which will prepare them to master the skill when they are older.*

+ *Be as concrete as possible. It's very easy to start talking about conflict in abstract terms, but this goes over the heads of young children. Discuss conflict in terms of specific actions and objects, and then move to more abstract aspects, such as motivation and point of view.*

+ *Help children see cause and effect. Primary grade children need to understand the relationship between cause and effect, a relationship that is central to resolving conflict. When discussing actual or hypothetical conflicts with children, help them to see the whole problem and how specific actions and behaviors contributed to it.*

+ *Strive to expand children's choices. Young children tend to have a limited array of conflict resolution approaches, and they will try to apply them to all conflicts, regardless of the potential consequences. Gently help them to see that there are other options. For example, sometimes during a discussion a child will insist that violence is the only solution to a conflict. ("I'd kick his head.") Help the child to understand the consequences of that action. ("If you kick his head, that will hurt him and you might get into trouble.") Then present some alternatives.*

*For a more detailed discussion of developmental considerations in teaching conflict resolution to primary grade children, see Nancy Carlsson-Paige and Diane E. Levin, "Making Peace in Violent Times: A Constructivist Approach to Conflict Resolution," *Young Children*, November, 1992.

Let's Get Started!

I've taught conflict resolution for many years in all kinds of settings—to all kinds of students. I have rarely met a child who was not, in some way, able to learn to be more effective at handling conflict. Because conflict is an essential part of children's lives, it's one of the most motivating topics you can teach. It's also a lot of fun. Children can use conflict resolution skills every day of their lives for the rest of their lives. By starting when children are young, we can get a head start on helping them acquire skills that will make a difference in their lives now, and will lead to a more peaceful world.

What's Conflict?

INTRODUCTION

When I asked a kindergarten class to tell me what conflict was, they responded enthusiastically. Conflict, they told me, was "kicking, hitting, pushing, scratching, punching, and slapping." They added solemnly, "But only babies bite."

Most primary grade children will say that conflict is a fight, by which they mean a physical fight. One result of this narrow definition is that many children do not even realize that they are in a conflict until it becomes a fight, which is an extreme form of conflict. It's easier to deal with a conflict before it becomes a physical fight, so the first step in helping children learn to resolve conflict is to expand their personal definitions of conflict. The activities and books in this chapter focus on the following concepts:

+ *Conflict is part of life and part of friendship.*

+ *Conflict has different forms.*

+ *There are many words to describe conflicts.*

INTRODUCTORY ACTIVITY

What's Conflict?

Objectives:

+ *to define conflict*
+ *to broaden children's understanding of conflict beyond "a fight"*

Materials:

Cardboard strip showing the word *conflict*
Conflict Discussion Pictures 1-3

SUGGESTED PROCEDURE

1 Display the cardboard strip, read the word *conflict* aloud, and ask if anyone knows what it means. Build on the students' responses by explaining that a conflict is a disagreement between people.

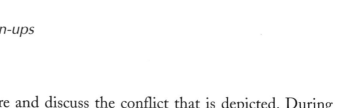

Questions for Discussion

+ *What is an example of a conflict?*

+ *What kinds of conflicts have you been in?*

+ *What do you think of when you hear the word conflict?*

+ *What kinds of conflicts do grown-ups have?*

2 Show each Conflict Discussion Picture and discuss the conflict that is depicted. During the discussion, encourage children to use words other than *fight* by modeling a range of conflict-related vocabulary.

Questions for Discussion

+ *What is happening in this picture?*

+ *What do you think the conflict is about?*

+ *How do you think the people in the conflict feel right now? How do you know?*

+ *What words would you use to describe this conflict?*

3 Have children draw a picture of a conflict they were involved in. Ask them to label the pictures, or dictate labels to you.

EXTENSION ACTIVITIES

Developing Conflict Vocabulary

Materials:

   Chart paper
   Markers

Create a *Conflict Words* chart to post in a prominent place. Begin with the words generated during the previous discussion. Add more words to the chart as they come up during the other activities in this book. As you add words, discuss their meanings. Try to use the words from the chart during discussions about conflict, and refer to the chart.

Conflict Web Chart

Materials:

   Chalkboard and chalk or newsprint and markers

Build on the first activity by creating a web chart. Write the word *conflict* on the board or on newsprint. Draw a ring around it. Have the children brainstorm words related to conflict. Record each suggestion and draw a line from the word to *conflict*. Words that are related to previous contributions can be linked to each other.

hitting
pushing } fight ——— (C O N F L I C T)
biting

won't share
|
shouting — arguments

friends
|
don't get along — calling names

being mean

CLASSROOM APPLICATIONS

Using Conflict Vocabulary

Look for opportunities to label conflicts and reinforce the concept that a conflict can be something other than a fight. Students will become more comfortable with the vocabulary of conflict when you model its use. Try to point out situations when classroom conflicts can be constructive or valuable. For example, "Tanesha and Jerome had a conflict in the block corner and they figured out a way to share."

Class Meetings

Class meetings provide an excellent forum for discussing conflict, solving problems, and teaching new skills. As children become familiar with the idea of conflict, have them describe conflicts they've observed around the school. How did the conflicts start? Did they get better or worse? Did the participants solve the conflict? What were the consequences of the conflict?

SUGGESTED LITERATURE

 *Let's Be Enemies,* by Janice May Udry
New York: HarperCollins, 1961

Summary

John and James have been friends for a long time, but when John decides he is fed up with James' bossy ways, he declares that they are enemies.

Before You Read

Explain that *Let's Be Enemies* is the story of two friends who have some conflicts.

- ✦ *Have you ever had a conflict with a good friend?*
- ✦ *What kinds of things do friends have conflicts about?*

As You Read

Stop after the second page.

- ✦ *How do you know the boys are having a conflict.*
- ✦ *What feelings do the boys have?*
- ✦ *How do you know?*

Stop at the sentence: *So now James is my enemy.*

- ✦ *Why is the boy mad at James?*
- ✦ *What are some of the things James does?*

Stop at the sentence: *GOOD-BYE!*

◆ *What happened with this conflict?*

◆ *What do you think the boys will do now?*

After You Read

◆ *How did John and James solve their conflict?*

◆ *Do you think they had more conflicts? What kinds?*

◆ *Describe a conflict you've had with a friend. How did you look during the conflict?*

FOLLOW-UP TO *LET'S BE ENEMIES*

Enemies and Friends

Materials:
Activity Sheet 1-1
Crayons

Using Activity Sheet 1-1, have the children draw pictures of John and James as enemies and as friends. Follow-up by having them draw and label pictures of themselves and a friend, first as enemies, and then as friends. Share the drawings. Continue the discussion concerning the types of conflicts friends have, how they look and feel during conflict, and how they resolve conflicts.

 *Three Wishes,* by Lucille Clifton
New York: Dell Yearling, 1974

Summary

When Nobie finds a penny on New Year's Day with her birthday year, it seems as though the penny makes her wishes come true. But the penny also leads to conflict between Nobie and her best friend.

Before You Read

Materials:
Penny

Tell your students that *Three Wishes* tells the story of a girl whose wishes lead to conflict with her best friend. Have the children sit in a circle. Hold up a penny and ask the children to pretend it is a magic penny that will grant wishes.

◆ *If you could wish for anything you wanted, what would you wish for? Have the children pass the penny and describe their wishes.*

As You Read

Stop at the point where Victor leaves the room.

> ✦ *What caused their conflict?*

> ✦ *What do you think will happen next?*

After You Read

Draw a "WWWWWH Chart" on the board, based on Chart 1-1. Discuss the conflict in the book, filling in the chart as you do. This activity will introduce the WWWWWH Chart for use with other books. The WWWWWH Chart helps children identify the basic facts about a conflict.

> ✦ *Who was involved?*

> ✦ *What was the conflict about?*

> ✦ *When did it happen?*

> ✦ *Where did it happen?*

> ✦ *Why was there a conflict?*

> ✦ *How did the conflict turn out?*

> ✦ *How might this conflict have been prevented?*

FOLLOW-UP TO *THREE WISHES*

My Friend and I Books

Materials:

> Activity Sheet 1-2
> Crayons

Discuss friendship by having children complete the sentence *Something I like to do with my friend is...* Ask volunteers to tell about conflicts they have had with friends. Build on the friendship discussion by using Activity Sheet 1-2. Have children complete the sentences and illustrate the pages of the book. Younger students can dictate sentences to you. Then have them cut and fold the Activity Sheet as directed to make a book.

Magic Penny Murals

Materials:

> Penny for each child
> Mural paper
> Crayons
> Glue

This activity builds on the pre-reading discussion. Have each child glue a penny to the mural paper and then draw a picture of a wish.

The Honey Hunters, by Francesca Martin
Cambridge: Candlewick Press, 1992

Summary

The honey guide is an African bird who promises a boy and a group of jungle animals that he will lead them to a delicious honeycomb. The animals then discover that sharing the honey is impossible.

Before You Read

Tell your students that *The Honey Hunters* is a tale that explains why some animals are enemies. Explain that some folktales provide explanations for why things are the way they are. There are tales that explain why zebras have stripes, why the sun is in the sky, and why mosquitos buzz in people's ears.

After You Read

+ *How did the boy distribute the honey? Do you think it was fair?*

+ *What did the animals do that made their conflict get worse?*

+ *What did the elephant mean when he said, "The damage is done"?*

+ *What do you think will happen to the animals who are left?*

FOLLOW-UP TO *THE HONEY HUNTERS*

A Different Ending

Have children pantomime the animals in *The Honey Hunters* as you read the story aloud. Stop reading just before the end, and have the role-players act out how the story might have ended if the animals agreed to share the honey.

What's Fair?

Materials:

Packaged cookies of a uniform size and shape (fifteen cookies for each group of four children)

Divide children into cooperative groups of three or four. Explain that you are the cookie bird and you will give each group some cookies. They must share the cookies in a way that feels fair to everyone in the group. Emphasize that they do not want to act like the animals in *The Honey Hunters*. After the groups have finished, ask them to describe how they shared the cookies and how they decided the method was fair. When the discussion is finished, they may eat the cookies.

ADDITIONAL BOOKS FOR IDENTIFYING CONFLICTS

Stevie, by John Steptoe. (New York: Harper Trophy, 1969)
> An older boy has conflicts with a younger boy named Stevie, until he realizes that Stevie needs him.

Swimmy, by Leo Lionni. (New York: Alfred E. Knopf, 1963)
> The little fish are in conflict with the big fish until Swimmy organizes them.

The Tale of Peter Rabbit, by Beatrix Potter. (New York: Frederic Warne, 1906)
> In this classic, Peter Rabbit has conflicts with Mr. MacGregor.

BUILDING ON THE THEME

WWWWWH Charts

Have children use Chart 1-1 with any of the additional books suggested, or with books suggested in other chapters. It's helpful if you have modeled the process at least once, as suggested in the activity for *Three Wishes*. With nonreaders, create WWWWWH Charts on the board or on chart paper, and complete them with the class.

Conflict Mural

When the class is familiar with a number of stories and conflicts, have groups of children create murals that illustrate conflict scenes from various books.

Enemies and Friends

James and John as enemies.	James and John as friends.
Me and _____ as enemies.	Me and _____ as friends.

 CHART 1-1

WWWWWH Chart

W Who was involved?

W What was the conflict about?

W When did it happen?

W Where did it happen?

W Why was there a conflict?

H How did the conflict turn out?

My Friend and I Book. *Let's Be Enemies,* by Janice May Udry

ε

2

My friend and I having a conflict...

My friend and I are doing
something we both like to do...

My friend and I resolving
our conflict...

_____

_____

My Friend and I

by _____

4

1

fold

fold

cut

cut

CHAPTER 2

The Conflict Escalator

INTRODUCTION

Anthony was one of my second-grade students. One day an angry cafeteria aide brought him to me. He'd been fighting again. "Anthony, what happened?" I asked. "I couldn't help it," he said shamefacedly. "I got on that Conflict Escalator and I just couldn't get off."

When conflicts get worse, we say that they escalate; if they get better, we say they de-escalate. The Conflict Escalator that Anthony referred to is a technique to diagram conflicts in a step-by-step manner. Each behavior of the disputants is a step on the escalator, either up or down. Children use the Conflict Escalator to record this behavior, and learn why conflicts escalate.

Unfortunately, many children do not even recognize that they are in a conflict until it has escalated. For these children—the Anthonys of the world—conflict feels more like an express elevator than an escalator. The Conflict Escalator helps children to understand how and why conflicts get worse. This is a key step in learning how to de-escalate conflicts, and how to control behavior in conflict situations.

The activities and books in this chapter focus on the following concepts:

✦ *Conflicts can be mapped on the Conflict Escalator.*

✦ *Identifiable behaviors contribute to conflict escalation.*

INTRODUCTORY ACTIVITIES

Conflict Escalates

Objectives:

+ *to introduce and use the Conflict Escalator*

+ *to identify behaviors that make a conflict escalate*

Materials:

Conflict Discussion Pictures 4-7
Chalkboard and chalk

SUGGESTED PROCEDURE

1 Ask the children to describe an escalator. If necessary, explain that an escalator is a set of stairs that moves up or down. Draw the following escalator graphic on the board:

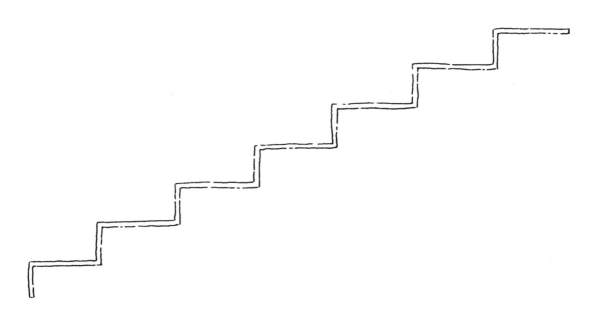

Explain that when conflicts get worse, we say that the people involved are on the *Conflict Escalator.*

2 Read the following story to the class as you show the appropriate Conflict Discussion Pictures:

Conflict Discussion Picture 4

Marcus and Stephanie were making masks. Their teacher, Ms. Chen, put some markers, paste, colored feathers, and sequins on the table. Stephanie took three big yellow feathers and five small red feathers. "I'm going to put these on my mask," she said.

Conflict Discussion Picture 5

"Hey!" said Marcus. "I was going to use them." Stephanie said, "I got them first." "You should share," said Marcus. Stephanie said, "I need them all. You just want them because I got them. You can use the green feathers or the sequins."

Conflict Discussion Picture 6

"I want to use those feathers," said Marcus, and he grabbed the yellow feathers away from Stephanie. "Give them to me," Stephanie yelled, and she pulled at the feathers.

Conflict Discussion Picture 7

The feathers broke into pieces. "Look what you did," said Marcus. "You wreck everything." "I'm telling," said Stephanie, and she went to get Ms. Chen.

3 Discuss the conflict as suggested below and map the conflict onto the Conflict Escalator:

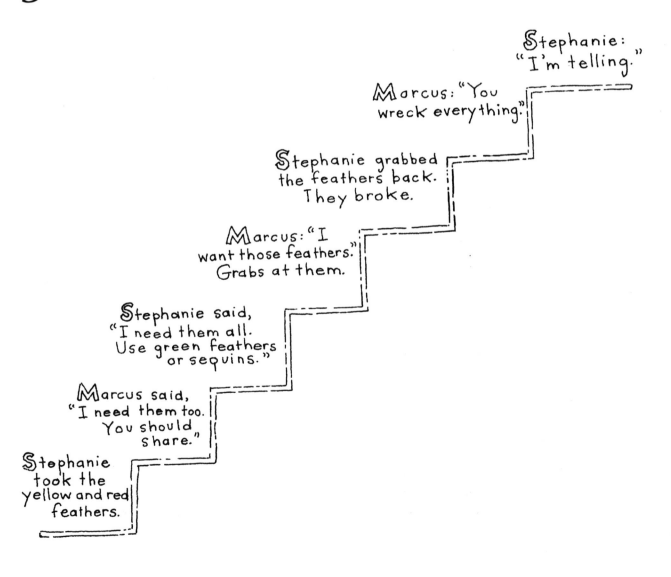

Questions for Discussion

♦ *What did Marcus and Stephanie say that made them go up the escalator?*

♦ *How could they have come down the escalator and solved their problem?*

♦ *What do you think Ms. Chen said to them?*

Using the Escalator

Objectives:

♦ **to practice mapping conflicts
on the Conflict Escalator**

♦ **to identify escalating behaviors**

Materials:
Activity Sheet 2-1
Scissors
Crayons
Glue
Drawing paper

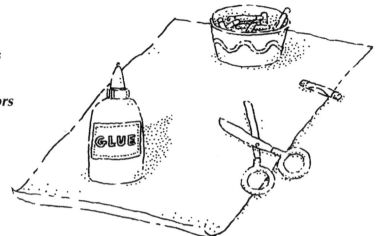

1 Divide students into cooperative groups of two or three, and distribute the materials. Help the children draw an escalator with four steps large enough to accommodate the pictures on Activity Sheet 2–1. Then read the following story to the class. As you read, have the children identify the appropriate illustrations.

> While Daniel was getting his snack out of the coat closet, his lunchbox accidentally fell and clunked Giorgio on the head. "Ow!" said Giorgio, rubbing his head. "You should be careful, you big jerk."
>
> Daniel felt bad about hitting Giorgio, but he didn't like being called a jerk. It was an accident! "Don't be such a baby. You shouldn't get in the way," said Daniel. Giorgio felt really angry. As Daniel bent over to pick up his lunchbox, Giorgio kicked it into the classroom.
>
> Mr. Avazian, their teacher, came back to the coat closet. "What's all this shouting about?" he asked. Daniel and Giorgio pointed at each other. "He started it!" they both said.

Questions for Discussion

♦ *What was the first thing that happened in this conflict?*

♦ *Which picture represents that? Where would you place it on the conflict escalator?*

♦ *What is the top of this conflict escalator?*

♦ *What made this conflict worse?*

- ✦ *What do you think the boys did after that?*
- ✦ *How do you think they solved their problem?*
- ✦ *How would you help them solve their problem?*

2 Have the children color the pictures, cut them out, and paste them onto the steps of the escalator in the correct sequence.

EXTENSION ACTIVITIES

Brainstorming Escalating Behaviors

Materials:

Chart paper

Have students identify the behaviors that contribute to conflict escalating by asking "When you are in a conflict, what are the things that make you go up the Conflict Escalator?" Write their contributions on a sheet of chart paper labeled *Things That Send Us Up the Conflict Escalator.*

A useful follow-up is to have children identify one of these behaviors that they will try to eliminate for an entire week. Make a poster titled *Stay Off the Conflict Escalator. Try not to* _____ *this week!* In the blank space, tape a card with the behavior of the week.

CLASSROOM APPLICATIONS

Using the Conflict Escalator

The Conflict Escalator is a tremendously useful concept to help children understand conflict and take responsibility for their behaviors. Make an effort to incorporate it into daily life in the classroom. When the children have conflicts, ask, "How did you get onto the Conflict Escalator? What sent you up the Conflict Escalator? How could you come down the Conflict Escalator?"

If you have a conflict with a child, you might say, "I think you and I are on the Conflict Escalator. How are we going to get off?"

SUGGESTED LITERATURE

 Matthew and Tilly, by Rebecca C. Jones
New York: Dutton Children's Books, 1991

Summary
Matthew and Tilly are good friends who share many adventures. But sometimes they have conflicts that ultimately lead to a stronger friendship.

Before You Read
Explain that *Matthew and Tilly* is a book about two friends who sometimes have conflicts when they play together. Have children sit in a circle. Go round the circle and have the children respond to the question, "What are some of the things that you and your friends like to do together?"

As You Read
Stop at the end of the page that begins: *Tilly found a piece of chalk...*

- ✦ *What is the conflict in the story?*
- ✦ *Did the conflict go up the escalator?*

Both go off alone.

Tilly: "You're stupid, stinky, and mean."

Matthew: "You're picky, stinky, mean."

Tilly: "No it wasn't. You always break everything."

Matthew: "It was old. It was ready to break."

Tilly: "You broke my crayon."

Matthew broke Tilly's crayon.

Discuss how the conflict escalated, and then continue the story by saying, "Let's see how Matthew and Tilly come down the Conflict Escalator."

After You Read

Re-read the escalation segment that begins: *Sometimes though, Matthew and Tilly got sick of each other*. Draw an escalator on the board (see page 30) as you discuss how to map this conflict on the Conflict Escalator.

- ✦ *What did Matthew and Tilly say to each other that made their conflict get worse?*
- ✦ *What would you say to Matthew and Tilly to help them come down the escalator?*
- ✦ *Have you ever had a conflict with a good friend? What happened?*

FOLLOW-UP TO *MATTHEW AND TILLY*

Friendly Animals

Materials:

Stuffed animals

Discuss the types of conflicts that children have with their friends. Ask pairs of children to choose two stuffed animals and act out an imaginary conflict between them. Then have them show how the animals resolve the conflict. You may wish to have other children watch the skit and discuss the conflict and resolution.

The Owl and the Woodpecker, by Brian Wildsmith
Oxford: Oxford University Press, 1971

Summary

When the owl moves into a new home, he does not realize that the woodpecker will hammer all day while he is trying to sleep. As the conflict between the owl and the woodpecker escalates, more and more animals get involved.

Before You Read

Discuss the different habits of owls and woodpeckers. Explain that owls sleep during the day and hunt for small animals at night. Woodpeckers sleep at night and search for insects during the day by pecking at tree bark. Both owls and woodpeckers build their nests in hollow trees. Ask: How could this lead to conflicts between owls and woodpeckers? Explain that *The Owl and the Woodpecker* tells of just such a conflict.

After You Read

Draw an escalator on the board and map the conflict on it.

- ✦ *What made the conflict escalate between the Owl and the Woodpecker?*

◆ *What happened to the conflict when all the other animals got involved?*

◆ *How do you think the Owl and Woodpecker were feeling during their conflict?*

◆ *When you are in a conflict, what are some of the things that send you up the escalator?*

FOLLOW-UP TO *THE OWL AND THE WOODPECKER*

Up and Down the Conflict Escalator

Materials:
    Activity Sheet 2-2
    Drawing paper
    Scissors
    Glue

Conflicts escalate or de-escalate because of the behaviors of the people involved. Refer to the chart the class made and discuss what behaviors in the story sent the conflict up and down the Conflict Escalator. Divide the children into cooperative groups of three or four and distribute the materials. Have the children cut out the boxes and glue the labels *Up the Escalator* and *Down the Escalator* at the top of the paper. Then ask them to decide whether the statement in each box represent something that sent the Owl and the Woodpecker up or down the escalator. Once they have decided, they glue each box under the appropriate label. For non-readers, make this a whole class activity where you read the statements aloud and the class decides where they should be placed.

 **The Pig War,** by Betty Baker
New York: HarperCollins, 1969

Summary

American farmers and British traders live together on an island. One day the Americans shoot a British pig, and a war begins. The pig war continues to escalate until the participants realize that the war is hurting both sides.

Before You Read

Hold up the book, read the title, and ask what a pig war might be. Read the first page aloud and talk about how the conflict might escalate. Explain that they may be surprised to hear how a small conflict can escalate into a big one.

After You Read

◆ *How did the pig war go up the Conflict Escalator?*

◆ *What things did the people say and do that made the conflict go up the escalator?*

◆ *If you were going to help Jed and the Captain make peace, how would you do it?*

FOLLOW-UP TO *THE PIG WAR*

Escalator Events

Materials:

Activity Sheet 2-3
Drawing paper
Scissors
Glue
Crayon or pencil

Divide the children into cooperative groups of two or three and distribute the materials. Have the children cut out the strips and order them in the correct story sequence. Next, have the children draw escalator steps and glue each strip onto the appropriate step. For non-readers, do this activity as a whole class activity as you read each strip aloud and the children tell you where the strips go.

ADDITIONAL BOOKS FOR THE CONFLICT ESCALATOR

It's Mine!, Leo Lionni (New York: Alfred A. Knopf, 1985).
Three frogs are in continual conflict over who owns the pond.

The Quarreling Book, by Charlotte Zolotow (New York: HarperCollins, 1963).
One day an entire family gets onto the Conflict Escalator.

Who's In Rabbit's House?, edited by Verna Aardema (New York: Dial Books for Young Readers, 1977). Someone is in Rabbit's house and the other animals try to get whoever-it-is out.

BUILDING ON THE THEME

Escalator Murals

Materials:

Mural paper
Drawing paper

Crayons
Glue

Divide children into cooperative groups of three or four. As a group they choose a book and draw pictures that illustrate events in the key conflict in the book. When the pictures are complete, have the children label them and glue them in sequence on a large escalator drawn on the mural paper. You may need to help the children divide the labor and decide who will draw each picture.

Book Posters

Materials:

Large sheets of drawing paper or poster board
Crayons

Have children create posters based on the theme of avoiding conflict escalating behaviors. These posters can feature characters from books they have read or discussed in class. For example, a poster featuring Clifford the Big Red Dog might say *Clifford says: "Don't call people names."*

The Owl and the Woodpecker, by Brian Wildsmith

Up the Escalator	**Down the Escalator**
The Owl screeched, "How can I possibly sleep with all that noise?"	**The mouse said, "Keep on tapping, Mister Woodpecker."**
The bear said, "Stop tapping, Woodpecker, and let the Owl sleep."	**The Owl asked the other animals for advice.**
The animals suggested that the Owl could move to another tree.	**"We will have to push the tree down to make the Owl move," said the fox.**
The Woodpecker tapped loudly so the Owl would know the tree was falling.	**The Owl thanked the Woodpecker.**

The Pig War, by Betty Baker

The bagpipes scared the pigs.

American soldiers came and marched up and down on the beach.

The farmer shot the pig.

The pigs went into the farmer's garden and wrecked it.

The farmers put up the flag and played a fiddle.

The soldiers put up the flag and played the bagpipes.

British warships came to the harbor.

Solving Conflicts

INTRODUCTION

I remember a discussion we had about the block corner when I was teaching kindergarten. We were discussing ways to share the blocks when one of the children, Carolyn, sighed, "Share, share, share. Grown-ups always say share. I hate sharing." I happen to think that sharing has a lot to recommend it, but I sympathize with Carolyn. Adults often get stuck by recommending only one or two ways to handle conflicts: *Share; just stay away from each other for a while.*

We forget that people use many approaches for handling and resolving conflicts. Young children tend to have only a few of these strategies at their commands. One goal of conflict resolution in the primary grades is to expand the number of choices children have in conflict situations. A way to do this is to model constructive, nonviolent conflict resolution. Another way is to help children explore different ways to handle conflicts. A third way is to help children practice the skills they need to de-escalate conflicts.

The activities and books in this chapter focus on the following concepts:

✦ *Various strategies for de-escalating and resolving conflict can be identified.*

✦ *Conflict resolution techniques need to be modeled.*

✦ *Skills related to conflict de-escalation need to be practiced.*

INTRODUCTORY ACTIVITIES

Coming Down the Escalator

Objectives:

+ *to discuss how to de-escalate conflict*

+ *to introduce the concept that there are many ways to solve conflicts*

Materials:

Conflict Discussion Picture 8

SUGGESTED PROCEDURE

1 Show Conflict Discussion Picture 8 and have the children describe the conflict depicted. Read the following story:

> Amos and Steve were working on a design on the computer. They weren't finished when Carmelita and Angela came over. "You guys have been on the computer forever," said Carmelita. "It's our turn now." "We're not finished yet," said Amos. "Stop bothering us so we can get this done." "Come on!" yelled Angela. "You guys always hog the computer. You're so selfish." "You're always bugging us," said Amos.

Questions for Discussion

+ *What's the conflict in this picture and story?*

+ *How do the boys feel? How do the girls feel? How can you tell?*

+ *What did they say to each other that made their conflict go up the escalator?*

+ *Do you think the boys have a right to finish their design?*

2 Discuss how the children in the story might solve their conflict. Write the suggestions on the board. If necessary, suggest some of the following:

The children set a timer to show how much longer the boys can have the computer.

The children apologize for hurtful things they've said.

The teacher gives the boys five more minutes.

The boys save their design on a disk and come back later.

The girls find something else to do.

3 When the brainstorm is complete, read the following ending to the story:

> "Well, it's not true that we always hog the computer," said Steve.

"But you've been on a long time today and we want to use it," said Angela.

"But we're almost finished with this," said Amos. "Can we just finish it and print it out?"

"Do you promise to give us the computer the second you finish?"

"Promise." And all the children shook hands.

Discuss the solution and ask the children if the solution seems fair.

Conflict Resolution Chart

Objectives

♦ *to identify common non-violent conflict resolution techniques*

Materials:

Chart 3–1
Chart paper

SUGGESTED PROCEDURE

Note: There's a lot for young children to absorb in this lesson. You may want to spread it out over several days.

1 Ask the children to brainstorm all the peaceful ways that people can solve conflicts. Record these ideas on the board or a sheet of newsprint. Then discuss the list by asking for examples of each conflict resolution approach. Remind the children that you are looking for ways to resolve conflict that don't hurt others.

2 Enlarge the Conflict Resolution Chart on a copier, or copy it onto chart paper. Display the chart and discuss each item on the list, comparing the chart to the list that the children developed. If there are any new or confusing terms, ask the class to describe examples.

Talk It Out—Many conflicts can be solved by sitting down and talking about the problem.

Listen to Each Other—People in the conflict need to be willing to listen to each other. Good listening helps each person understand what the other is thinking and feeling.

Share—If people are having a conflict about who gets to use something, there may be a way to use the object at the same time.

Take Turns—One way to share is to decide that first one person uses it, and then the other person has a turn.

Compromise—If both people give in a little, they compromise.

Make a Peace Offering—One person gives a little gift or something that shows he or she wants to solve the conflict.

Say "I'm Sorry"—*Sorry* can mean different things. One reason to say *sorry* is when you are wrong. It can also be a way of saying, "I feel bad we're having this conflict."

Build Trust—Sometimes one person doesn't believe what the other says. People need to trust each other.

Work Together—Sometimes a conflict can be solved by agreeing to work together on a project or idea.

Solve the Problem—Conflicts are problems. If the people solve the problem, then the conflict will be solved.

Put It Off—Sometimes people are too angry to talk it out or solve the problem. They may need to take a break and work on it later.

Skip It—Some conflicts aren't worth bothering with. Just forget about it.

Get Help—Sometimes you can't come to a solution by yourselves, and you need to ask a grown-up or another child to help you.

Questions for Discussion

✦ *Can you give an example of a time you used any of these ideas?*

✦ *What happened?*

EXTENSION ACTIVITY

Good Listening

Discuss why listening is important. For example, by listening we get information, learn things, identify dangerous situations, learn how others feel, and get enjoyment. Arrange for one child to help you demonstrate poor listening and good listening. Say the following to the child:

_____(Child's name), I just got a message from the principal. You won a million dollars and a free trip to Mexico. But you have to go down to the office right away and call the contest people, or they will give the prize to someone else. You have to say these special words to them or they will give the prize to someone else. You have to say, "I'm a great listener." Do you understand?

As you talk, have the child look around the room, fidget, interrupt, hum, and show other signs of poor listening. Ask the children to describe what they saw. Then repeat the speech and have the child demonstrate good listening by paying attention, looking at you, nodding occasionally, and repeating the key information when you have said, "Do you understand?"

✦ *What did you see the second time?*

✦ *How was it different from the first time?*

◆ *What did _____ lose out on because of poor listening?*

◆ *How could good listening help you in a conflict?*

CLASSROOM APPLICATIONS

The Conflict Resolution Chart

The Conflict Resolution Chart can be a useful tool in the classroom. Post it in a prominent place and refer to it often. If two children have a conflict, you might intervene by asking which of the conflict resolution methods on the chart they would like to use. Similarly, when you intervene in conflicts, point out methods you are using.

New Approaches

One of the goals of this chapter is to encourage children to expand the conflict resolution choices and options they use. Try some new approaches yourself. For example, if you find yourself constantly telling children to share, try giving them the responsibility for solving the problem by asking them to talk it out and come up with a solution. The solution they come up with may well be to share, but the process will help children develop and internalize conflict resolution skills.

Here's a simple technique for encouraging children to use the techniques on the Conflict Resolution Chart. Keep a timer on your desk. When they come to you with a conflict, or when you interrupt one in progress, ask them to choose a method from the chart. Set the timer for three minutes. Assure them that after three minutes you will help, but they should try to work it out themselves. Often they will be able to work it out, and your role can change from arbitrator to time keeper!

Evaluating the Conflict Resolutions

After children have tried a conflict resolution approach, help them evaluate it. For example, during a class meeting time you might ask them to describe what they did and how it worked. This gives children an opportunity to reflect on their actions, and acknowledge success, and it helps other children learn how to use the conflict resolution methods in real-life situations.

SUGGESTED LITERATURE

 *The Knight and the Dragon,* by Tomie dePaola
New York: G.B. Putnam's Sons, 1980

Summary

A knight and a dragon decide to have a fight. They prepare carefully, and on the scheduled day they go through with their duel. With help, they figure out a way to make peace.

Before You Read

Explain that *The Knight and the Dragon* tells how someone helped solve a conflict. Ask the children to talk about conflicts when they needed help. Who helped? What did they do or say to help solve the conflict?

As You Read

Much of *The Knight and the Dragon* is wordless. Have children describe the action in the pictures. After the fight begins, show the two-page illustration that depicts the knight and the dragon charging each other.

- *What do you think will happen next?*
- *How could the knight and the dragon solve their conflict?*

After some discussion, finish the story.

After You Read

Discuss the story and map it on a down escalator.

Questions for Discussion

- *Which methods from our chart did the knight and the dragon use?*
- *What do you think the woman said to them?*
- *What are some other things they might have done together besides fight?*

The knight and the dragon crashed.

The princess came and gave them books.

They read the books together.

They set up a restaurant.

The dragon cooks, the knight serves.

FOLLOW-UP TO *THE KNIGHT AND THE DRAGON*

Eyewitness News

Have three children act out the roles of the Knight, the Dragon, and the Princess. A fourth child plays the role of television news reporter for the six o'clock news. You may want to demonstrate the activity by playing the role of the reporter yourself. The reporter asks questions of the characters to find out the story of their conflict and how it was resolved. Other children may wish to continue the activity with characters from other stories.

 ## *The Island of the Skog,* by Steven Kellogg
New York: Dial Books, 1973

Summary

Frustrated by the dangers of urban life, a group of mice set sail on a model ship to search for a more peaceful place to live. They land on the Island of the Skog. No one is sure what a Skog is, but judging from its footprints, they assume it must be huge and fierce.

Before You Read

Tell the children that *The Island of the Skog*, some mice meet a creature called a Skog. Ask the children what they do to get to know someone.

As You Read

Stop reading at the point where the Skog is approaching the honey jar. Don't show this picture to the children. Ask a few volunteers to come to the board and draw pictures showing what they think the Skog looks like. After they finish, continue the story.

After You Read

+ *Why was the Skog frightened of the mice?*

+ *What conflict resolution methods on our chart did the mice and the Skog use?*

+ *Louise suggested that they bring presents to the Skog to show that they were friendly. How might the story have changed if the mice brought the presents?*

FOLLOW-UP TO *THE ISLAND OF THE SKOG*

Story Puppets

Materials:
   Activity Sheet 3-1
   Craft sticks or strips of stiff cardboard
   Crayons

Have the children act out different endings to the story based on approaching someone they don't know in a friendly way. Have children make stick puppets by coloring the figures from Activity Sheet 3-1. Then have them cut out the figures and mount them on craft sticks or strips of stiff cardboard.

The figure of the Skog is ideal for making sock puppets. Have the children cut two circles of felt the size of nickels and glue them to the foot of a sock for eyes.

Angel Child, Dragon Child, by Michelle Maria Surat
New York: Scholastic, 1983

Summary

Ut has just come to the United States from Vietnam, and she does not like her new American school. The children laugh when she speaks, a bully named Raymond picks on her, and most of all, she misses her mother in Vietnam. Eventually Ut solves her problems and, to her surprise, befriends the bully.

Before You Read

Angel Child, Dragon Child is about a girl named Ut who is teased in her new school. Ask about how it feels to be teased.

As You Read

Stop reading at the end of page 19.

> ✦ *What do you think will happen next?*
>
> ✦ *How could Ut and Raymond solve their conflict?*

After You Read

> ✦ *What methods from our chart did Ut and Raymond use? (Talk it out; Listen; Peace offering)*
>
> ✦ *Do you think the other children were kind to Ut? Why or why not?*
>
> ✦ *If you were teased by a bully, what could you do?*

FOLLOW-UP TO *ANGEL CHILD, DRAGON CHILD*

Conflict Stories

Materials:

   Cassette Player

Ask the children to name some of their favorite book characters. Have pairs of students think of a conflict story that involves some of these characters. Children then record their stories, focusing on the conflicts and the resolutions. Encourage other children to listen to the stories and discuss how the conflicts were solved. Encourage children to suggest different ways to solve the conflicts.

ADDITIONAL BOOKS FOR SOLVING CONFLICTS

Babar and the Wully-Wully, by Laurent De Brunhoff. (New York: Random House, 1975)
>   When the cruel Rataxes kidnaps the gentle Wully-Wully, an old dispute between Babar and Rataxes flares up.

Clancy's Coat, by Eve Bunting (New York: Frederick Warne and Co., 1984)
>   Clancy and Tippet have been enemies, but through a series of peace offerings, they become friends again.

First Pink Light, by Eloise Greenfield (New York: Black Butterfly Children's Books, 1976)
>   A boy and his mother negotiate bedtime.

BUILDING ON THE THEME

Charting Conflict Resolution

Materials:
>   Chart 3-1

This activity may be done by individual students or by the whole class. Reproduce the chart. At the top, write the title of a book. Underneath the title, check the methods of conflict resolution that are used in the book.

How I Solved My Conflict

Have volunteers act out the parts of characters in books you have read to the class. The other children ask questions about the conflict and how it was resolved. The children try to guess who the character is. This activity works best if you model it once or twice.

Talk It Out

✦

Listen to Each Other

✦

Share

✦

Take Turns

✦

Compromise

✦

Make a Peace Offering

✦

Say "I'm Sorry"

✦

Build Trust

✦

Work Together

✦

Solve the Problem

✦

Put It Off

✦

Skip It

✦

Get Help

Cut out along the dotted lines.

CHAPTER 4

Solving Problems

INTRODUCTION

Most conflict resolution is based on problem solving. One of my students once wrote, "I like problem solving. Sometimes it doesn't work. And sometimes it's like magic. I like the magic." The *magic* happens when conflicts are resolved in a way that leads to what we call *win–win* resolutions, resolutions that meet the needs of all the people involved.

Many children see conflict as a contest, where one party can only *win* if the other party *loses*. They are completely unfamiliar with the idea that all parties can *win*. Because of their ages and because they see very few models of win-win resolution, the concept can be particularly challenging for young children. In this chapter I have simplified the concept by referring to *Thumbs Up* and *Thumbs Down* solutions. The activities and books in this chapter focus on the following concepts:

- ✦ *Children learn a process of open-ended problem solving.*

- ✦ *Children can participate in win-win resolutions.*

- ✦ *Opportunities should be provided to practice problem-solving.*

- ✦ *Children can evaluate conflict solutions using the Thumbs Up /Thumbs Down model.*

INTRODUCTORY ACTIVITIES

The ABCD Conflict Solving Method

Objectives:

✦ *to introduce the ABCD Conflict Solving process*

✦ *to give children an opportunity to practice the ABCD Conflict Solving process*

Materials:
Chart 4–1

SUGGESTED PROCEDURE

1 Refer to the Conflict Resolution Chart from the previous chapter. Explain that many of the conflict resolution methods on the chart involve some kind of problem solving. Display the ABCD Conflict Solving Chart and discuss the steps on it with the class.

1) Ask, "What's the problem?"

2) Brainstorm some solutions.

3) Choose the best solution.

4) Do it.

2 Introduce the ABCD method by using the following story:

The children in Mr. Aronstein's class had been waiting for weeks for the new set of books for their class library. Finally the box arrived. The children gathered around as Mr. Aronstein opened the box and took out copies of seven new books. "I want the one on top," called Urvashi. "I want the other one," shouted Santel. All the children called out to be the first ones to read the books. "Quiet down, everyone, " said Mr. Aronstein. "Boy, we've got a problem," said Jim.

Questions for Discussion

✦ *What problem does Mr. Aronstein's class have?*

✦ *What are some ways they could solve this problem?*

✦ *Which solution do you think would be best?*

✦ *How could the class follow through on the solution?*

✦ *Have you ever worked out a conflict by following steps like these?*

Thumbs Up, Thumbs Down

Objectives:

✦ *to help students evaluate potential conflict solutions*

Materials:

Activity Sheet 4-1
Scissors

SUGGESTED PROCEDURE

1 Explain that when we are trying to resolve conflicts, some solutions are better than others. The best conflict solutions don't hurt anyone, and everybody involved in the conflict can say, "That's okay with me."

2 Show the group a thumbs up sign, and a thumbs down sign and discuss their meanings with the class. You may need to explain that they are ways of saying, *okay!* and *not okay!* Give each child a copy of Activity Sheet 4-1 and have them color and cut out the thumbs. Tape the tab at the bottom so that children can attach them to their thumbs for *thumbs up* and *thumbs down* signals.

3 Reassemble the group and have them evaluate the following conflict resolutions *thumbs up, thumbs down*. Present the situation:

In Ms. Lopez's classroom, the children love to put jigsaw puzzles together. There are ten boxes of puzzles. Lately they've found that pieces from different puzzles have been mixed together. Ms. Lopez gathered the class together and said, "We've got a problem. The puzzle pieces are getting mixed together."

Questions for Discussion

✦ *Why is this a problem for the class?*

✦ *How do you think the children felt when they tried to put puzzles together and found pieces that didn't belong?*

4 Ask the children to listen to all the solutions that the class thought of without evaluating them.

✦ *Ms. Lopez takes all the puzzles away and no one gets to use them.*

✦ *Ms. Lopez buys all new puzzles.*

✦ *Some children volunteer to sort the puzzle pieces.*

✦ *The class sets up a procedure for putting puzzles away so pieces don't get mixed up.*

✦ *Once the puzzle pieces are sorted, the back of the pieces are marked with a color to show where they belong.*

✦ *Everyone promises never to mix the puzzle pieces again.*

5 Go through the list again, asking children to evaluate the solutions as *thumbs up* or *thumbs down,* using their cardboard thumbs. For each solution, ask the children what the consequences or outcomes of the solution might be. Would it be thumbs up for everyone? Thumbs down for everyone? Thumbs up for some and thumbs down for others? Finish the activity by having the children identify which solutions are the most workable.

EXTENSION ACTIVITIES

Brainstorming

Materials:

An ordinary object, such as a box, a wooden spoon, or a cardboard tube

Brainstorming is a skill that should be practiced often, in all types of problem solving. Explain that the purpose of brainstorming is to come up with as many ideas as possible in a short period of time. During the brainstorm, no one says whether the ideas are good or bad, sensible or silly, workable or not workable. The point is simply to get out as many ideas as possible. After the brainstorm is finished, the ideas are evaluated.

Set the object in front of the class. Ask them to suggest all the things that they could do with that object. Write their suggestions on the board. After a few minutes, or after energy for the brainstorm runs down, end the brainstorm and begin evaluating the ideas. What does the class think it would like to do with the object? If at all possible, do what the class decides.

Thumbs Up/ Thumbs Down Chart

Materials:

Chart 4-2

This chart is used in the activities that follow. Introduce the Thumbs Up/ Thumbs Down Chart by explaining that it is a way to remember all the possible solutions in a conflict. As you explain the chart, point to the appropriate box and then use both hands to indicate thumbs up/thumbs down. Explain that some solutions make both people go thumbs up. Some solutions make one person go thumbs up and the other go thumbs down.

CLASSROOM APPLICATIONS

Class Problem Solving

Encourage a problem-solving frame of mind in the classroom by using the the ABCD Problem Solving Process and the Thumbs Up/ Thumbs Down Chart to solve a problem in the classroom. Have the children brainstorm a list of class problems. Then ask them to choose one and brainstorm ways to solve it. When the brainstorming is finished, discuss which ideas might be thumbs up solutions and discuss possible ways to implement the solutions.

Intervening in Conflicts

Help children become more comfortable with the language of problem solving by using it when you intervene in conflicts. You don't always need to use the entire ABCD method. You can simply help children identify what the problem is and then ask, "Can you think of a thumbs up solution to this conflict?" The more children hear this language, the more likely they will be to use it themselves.

SUGGESTED LITERATURE

"The Zax," by Dr. Seuss
Included in the book *The Sneetches,* New York: Random House, 1961

Summary
A North-going Zax and a South-going Zax run into each other. Each refuses to budge an inch in either direction, and so they are stuck.

Before You Read
"The Zax" is a story about two people in a face-to-face conflict. Have the children find partners and stand facing them. Ask them to show how they would look if they were having a conflict. The partners should not touch each other; they should show by facial expression and body stance how they would look.

As You Read
Stop reading after page 32. With the class, discuss how the Zax might solve their conflict in a thumbs up way. Encourage the children to come up with as many thumbs up solutions as possible. Then finish the story.

After You Read

+ *Did the story end with a thumbs up or a thumbs down solution?*

+ *How was the ending different from the ideas you had?*

+ *Have you ever been in a conflict where one person wouldn't budge? What did you do?*

FOLLOW-UP TO *"THE ZAX"*

Act Like a Zax

Have the children work in pairs. One child is designated the North-going Zax and the partner is the South-going Zax. Have them act out the conflict as you read the story aloud. Stop reading at the end of page 32 and ask them to demonstrate a thumbs up solution to the conflict. Finish the story and add the lines:

Oh those poor Zaxes.
They're both wearing frowns.
They could be thumbs up,
But instead they're thumbs down.

 ## *Six Crows,* by Leo Lionni
New York: Alfred A. Knopf, 1988

Summary
A farmer and a group of six crows are in dispute over a field of wheat. A wise owl helps them come up with a compromise.

Before You Read
Explain that *Six Crows* tells the story of a farmer who has conflicts with many crows. Ask the class to discuss conflicts that a farmer might have with a crow. What could a farmer and a crow say to each other?

As You Read
Stop reading at the end of the page where the owl says: *Words can do magic.* Have the children brainstorm possible solutions to the conflict, first by using the ABCD Conflict Solving process, and then evaluating the solutions as either thumbs up or thumbs down. Finish the story.

After You Read

+ *How did the farmer and the crows resolve their conflict?*

+ *What conflict resolution method from our chart did they use?*

+ *What did the owl mean when she said, "Words can do magic"?*

FOLLOW-UP TO *SIX CROWS*
Magic Words in Conflicts
Materials:
Activity Sheet 4-2 (cut into strips)
Drawing paper
Crayons
Scissors
Glue

Discuss the magic sentences on Activity Sheet 4-2. How might these sentences be helpful in conflict situations? Have children work in pairs and give each pair one of the magic sentence strips cut from Activity Sheet 4-2. Ask children to draw a picture that illustrates people using that magic sentence. They can glue the strip to the bottom of the picture.

Thumbs Up Collages

Materials:

> Drawing paper
> Scraps of colored paper
> Crayons
> Glue

Leo Lionni illustrated *Six Crows* using torn paper to create collages. Have the children use the same technique to make a mural showing the owl, the crows, the farmer, and the scarecrow after the Thumbs Up solution has been reached. This works best if children take one piece of colored scrap paper, glue it to the drawing paper, and then use crayons to draw the rest of the figure.

The Terrible Thing That Happened at My House,
by Marge Blaine. New York: Scholastic, 1975

Summary

When a girl's mother gets a job as a science teacher, everything in the family changes—for the worse. Finally the girl confronts her family, and they figure out win-win solutions to their problems.

Before You Read

Tell the children that *The Terrible Thing That Happened at My House* is the story of what happens when a family gets too busy to listen to each other. Discuss what happens when people don't listen to each other. For example, there can be misunderstandings, hurt feelings, etc.

As You Read

Stop reading at the end of the page with the sentence: *My parents really listened this time and then they said 'Let's see what we can do.'* Have the children describe the problem, and brainstorm possible solutions using the ABCD Conflict Solving process. Evaluate the solutions using Thumbs Up/ Thumbs Down.

After You Read

- ✦ *What methods from the Conflict Solving Chart did the family use to solve their problem?*
- ✦ *How did the parents let the girl know that they loved her?*
- ✦ *How do you solve problems in your family?*

✦ *If you were going help the family in the book solve their problem, what would you do?*

FOLLOW-UP TO *THE TERRIBLE THING THAT HAPPENED AT MY HOUSE*

Letter to the Family

Have the children write or dictate a letter to the family in *The Terrible Thing That Happened at My House* explaining the ABCD conflict solving method and suggesting thumbs up solutions for the problem.

ADDITIONAL BOOKS FOR PROBLEM SOLVING

The Big Pile of Dirt, by Eleanor Clymer. (New York: Holt, 1968)
   A group of city children discovers a vacant lot with a big pile of dirt, and they put it to good use. But the grown-ups have other plans for the lot.

Bootsie Barker Bites, by Barbara Bottner. (New York: G.P. Putnam's Sons, 1992)
   A little girl has to play with the terrifying Bootsie Barker until she learns to stand up to Bootsie.

The Butter Battle, by Dr. Seuss (New York: Random House, 1984)
   How should buttered bread be eaten? Two nations dispute this issue and keep building bigger weapons.

BUILDING ON THE THEME

Solve It with Puppets

Materials:

   Construction paper
   Craft sticks or strips of
   stiff cardboard

Have children make stick puppets of the main characters in a book they have read. When the puppets are complete, they can act out the main conflict of the book. Ask them to stop the presentation before they reach the resolution. The class can then use the ABCD approach to solve the problem for the puppets.

A New Ending

Materials:

  Activity Sheet 4-3
  Crayons
  Pencils

Have children use the Activity Sheet 4-3 to develop new endings to stories they have read. You may wish to do this as a whole class activity to model the process. Then have the children work in cooperative groups to complete the activity sheet and develop alternative endings. The completed sheets, with illustrations, can be bound into a book or posted on a bulletin board. With non-reading students, use the sheet as a discussion springboard and have them illustrate alternate endings.

CHART 4-1

ABCD Conflict Solving

A

Ask, "What's the problem?"

B

Brainstorm some solutions.

C

Choose the best solution.

D

Do it.

Thumbs Up/Thumbs Down Chart

Would everyone say "Thumbs Up"?

Would everyone say "Thumbs Down"?

Would some say "Thumbs Up" and some say "Thumbs Down"?

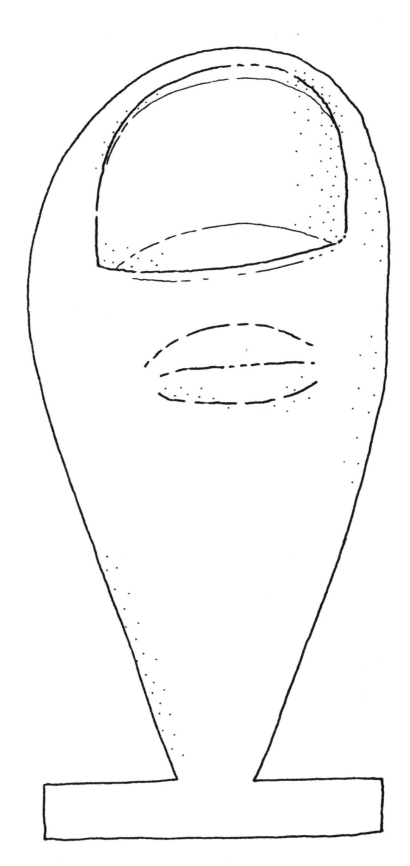

Let's work it out.

I'm sorry.

We can share.

I don't want to fight.

We can take turns.

We can solve this conflict.

Let's get someone to help us.

Book Title: _____

Author: _____

The main characters in the book were: _____

_____

The conflict they had was: _____

_____

_____

_____

_____

They solved the conflict by: _____

_____

_____

_____

_____

Some other ways they could solve the problem are: _____

_____

_____

_____

_____

Choose one of your solutions that you think is a Thumbs Up solution. Draw a picture of the characters solving their conflict that way.

CHAPTER 5

Understanding Other Perspectives

INTRODUCTION

When I was young and would get into conflicts with one of my three brothers, my grandmother would say, "There are two sides to every argument: yours, his, and what really happened." I have since learned that despite what's really happened, the heart of a conflict is the different perspectives on what happened. This is why there is a conflict in the first place.

Understanding other points of view is an essential skill in resolving conflict. Developmentally, it is also one of the most difficult. This is an area where you should think in terms of readiness, not mastery. My experience has been that while young children have difficulty adopting or even identifying the perspective of another person, they can prepare to do so through stories and activities that help them experiment with different points of view.

Introducing young children to the concept of perspective serves a readiness function, and it also shows children that understanding different perspectives is something that we value in our culture.

The activities and books in this chapter focus on the following concepts:

+ *Children can look at different points of view in a conflict.*

+ *Children can have experiences with the concept of point of view by presenting a unique perspective on the world.*

INTRODUCTORY ACTIVITIES

Do You See What I See?

Objectives:

> ✦ *to introduce the concept of point of view*

SUGGESTED PROCEDURE

1 Stand before the group and pantomime a simple activity, such as washing windows. Ask the children to guess what you're doing. Try to elicit several different guesses for the activity. For example, washing windows may look like waving to a friend or erasing the chalkboard. Point out that children saw the same activity differently.

2 Ask for a volunteer to stand before the group and act out an activity. It may be helpful to give suggestions for pantomimes, such as:

> ✦ *scrubbing the floor by hand;*
>
> ✦ *watching TV;*
>
> ✦ *talking on the phone;*
>
> ✦ *riding in the car and looking out the window;*
>
> ✦ *mixing cookie dough.*

3 Explain that the same activity can look different to other people. We all see the world differently. The way we see the world is called our *point of view.*

Points of View in Conflicts

Objectives:

> ✦ *to reinforce the concept of differing points of view*
>
> ✦ *to practice identifying different points of view*

Materials:

Two sets of adult-sized footprints, one set traced on red construction paper, the other set traced on blue construction paper

1 Remind the children that people have different ways of looking at things. Because we have different bodies, different families, and different experiences, we see the world differently. The way we see the world is called our *point of view.* When people have conflicts, they often see the problem differently. Ask the children to listen to the following situation and try to identify the point of view of each girl in the story:

Tamika and Dawn sat next to each other. One day, the class watched a video about dinosaurs. During the discussion, Tamika kept raising her hand to answer the teacher's questions. Tamika said to Dawn, "I love dinosaurs. I wish we always did dinosaurs in science." Dawn liked dinosaurs too, but she didn't know as much about them as Tamika. "You just like to show off. You think you know everything," said Dawn. "I'm not a show off," said Tamika. "You're just dumb."

2 Show the footprints and explain that the red footprints represent Tamika and the blue footprints represent Dawn. Set the footprints on the floor and ask for volunteers to stand on each set of prints and give the point of view of Tamika and Dawn.

Questions for Discussion

+ *How would Tamika describe the problem?*

+ *How would Dawn describe the problem?*

+ *If you were their teacher, how would you describe the problem?*

+ *What is a misunderstanding?*

+ *Why did Tamika and Dawn have a misunderstanding?*

+ *How could they solve their problem?*

3 Repeat the footprint exercise using the Conflict Discussion Pictures from Chapter 1. Show the pictures to the class and have volunteers stand in the footprints and give the appropriate points of view.

EXTENSION ACTIVITIES

POV Box

Materials:
A closed cardboard box with a hole cut in its side. Both the box and the hole should be large enough to fit child's hand inside. Place two common object in the box, such as a small stuffed animal, a square wooden block, a plastic bottle, a small ruler, a computer disk, a notepad, and a candle.

Explain that our point of view is not limited to what we see with our eyes. Our sense of touch also gives us information. Place two objects in the box. Have a volunteer put his or her hand in the box and try to identify the objects inside by touch. He or she should whisper the names to you. Then ask a second child to guess. Then discuss the guesses and the different points of view with the rest of the class. Repeat the activity with other objects and volunteers.

Gossip

Explain that sometimes people don't listen carefully or misunderstand what they hear, which might lead to conflict. Play the game *Gossip*. Whisper a message into a student's ear. He or she whispers the message to a second student, who passes the message to a third, and so on until everyone has heard the message. The last student repeats what he or she heard. Compare that message with the first message. Discuss how misunderstandings can lead to conflict. Possible example sentences are: 1) At lunch yesterday, two big kids had an argument and they decided to write about it. 2) Some kids made bubbles at recess and they have to stay in.

CLASSROOM APPLICATIONS

Identify and Articulate Points of View

Look for opportunities to identify points of view with the children by using the point of view footprints. For example, if two children have a conflict, ask them to stand on the point of view footprints and identify the problem. Then have them stand in the other person's footprints and restate the problem from that point of view. This will be difficult for younger children, but the goal is to begin developing a habit of looking at other points of view.

SUGGESTED LITERATURE

The Hating Book, by Charlotte Zolotow
New York: HarperCollins, 1969

Summary

One girl decides that she hates her friend because of a series of slights and insults. Finally, she gathers her courage and asks her friend why she's being so mean. It turns out there's another point of view on this misunderstanding.

Before You Read

Tell your students that *The Hating Book* is about two girls who have a misunderstanding. Ask if anyone has ever had a misunderstanding with a friend because of a different point of view. Encourage the children to listen for the different points of view in the story.

After You Read

You may want to use the point of view footprints from the introductory lesson. Have volunteers stand on the footprints and describe the misunderstanding from the point of view of one of the characters.

♦ *What was the first girl's point of view?*

- ✦ *What was the second girl's point of view?*
- ✦ *The mother kept saying, "Ask her why." Was that good advice?*
- ✦ *What conflict resolution did the girls use?*

FOLLOW-UP TO *THE HATING BOOK*

Talk Balloons

Materials:
- Activity Sheet 5-1
- Scissors
- Glue
- Drawing paper
- Crayons

Distribute a copy of Activity Sheet 5-1 to each child. Have them write a sentence in each thought balloon that represents the point of view of each girl in *The Hating Book*. Next, have the children draw pictures of each girl. When they have finished the pictures, they cut out each talk balloon and paste it by the appropriate figure.

You may wish to have non-writers dictate their sentences to you.

✦ *Tar Beach,* by Faith Ringgold
New York: Crown Publishers, 1991

Summary

Cassie Louise Lightfoot wants to be free to go wherever she wants. One night, on the roof of her apartment building, she finds that she can "fly" wherever she wants to go.

Before You Read

Explain that *Tar Beach* is the story of a girl who imagines that she can fly. Have the class sit in a circle and show them a feather. Explain that they are to pretend it's a magic feather and they can use it to fly anywhere in the world. Have the children pass the feather around the circle and complete the statement, "If I could fly, I would fly to..."

After You Read

- ✦ *Why did Cassie want to fly?*
- ✦ *What were some of the conflicts in the story?*
- ✦ *If you had Cassie for a friend, what would the two of you do?*

FOLLOW-UP TO *TAR BEACH*

Point of View Quilt

Materials:

Squares of light colored cloth for each child
Fabric crayons

Refer to the earlier discussion about flying. Ask the children to think about how things would look as they flew over them. Show children the last page of the book and explain that *Tar Beach* is based on a quilt made by the author/illustrator. Distribute fabric squares and crayons, and have the children draw themselves flying to a place they would like to go. Sew the squares together into a quilt.

A simpler version of this activity is to have children draw their pictures on drawing paper. Tape the pictures together to form a paper quilt.

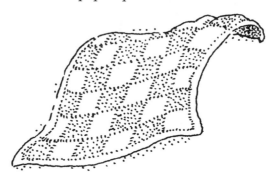

Here Comes the Cat!, by Frank Asch and Vladimir Vagin
New York: Scholastic, 1989

Summary

A community of mice is gripped with fear when they learn that a cat is coming. The fear and prejudice turn out to be unfounded—the cat comes in peace and friendship. The book is a collaboration between an American author/illustrator and a Russian artist.

Before You Read

Explain that in *Here Comes the Cat!* the class will meet some worried mice. Ask the children if they have ever worried about something that might happen. Ask them to listen for the point of view of the mice in the story.

As You Read

Stop halfway through the book.

◆ *What is the point of view of the mice?*

+ *Do you think their points of view will change?*

+ *What might make them change?*

After You Read

+ *How did the mouse point of view almost lead to a conflict?*

+ *What caused the mice to change their points of view?*

+ *Have you ever changed your point of view because of something that happened?*

FOLLOW-UP TO *HERE COMES THE CAT!*

The Cat Point of View

Materials:

Drawing paper

Crayons

Explain that *Here Comes the Cat!* was a collaboration between two artists from different countries. Have children work in cooperative groups to write and illustrate a version of *Here Comes the Cat!* told from the point of view of the cat. Encourage them to show how the cat plans the surprise for the mice, what she says to herself on the way to the village, her reactions to the mice, and so on.

ADDITIONAL BOOKS FOR POINT OF VIEW

Two Bad Ants, by Chris Van Allsburg. (Boston: Houghton Mifflin, 1988)
Two ants go exploring in the wide world. The story presents a fascinating depiction of the ants' view of the world.

The Chinese Mirror, by Mirra Ginsburg. (San Diego: Voyager/Harcourt Brace Jovanovich, 1988) A Korean folktale tells about a mirror that reflects a different point of view to everyone who looks in it.

The True Story of the Three Pigs by A. Wolf, by Jon Scieszka. (New York: Viking, 1989)
The story of the three pigs is told from the point of view of the wolf.

BUILDING ON THE THEME

Point of View Chart

Keep a Point of View Chart of the books the class reads, and use it to record differing points of view and how they lead to conflict. With the class, record the following information on the chart:

TITLE	CONFLICT	POINTS OF VIEW
The Hating Book by Charlotte Zolotow	One girl thought the other was mean.	Girl 1: She won't play with me. Girl 2: She said I looked like a freak.
The Island of the Skog by Steven Kellogg	The mice tried to attack the Skog.	Mice: If we don't attack the Skog he'll hurt us. Skog: The mice are trying to hurt me.

The Hating Book, by Charlotte Zolotow

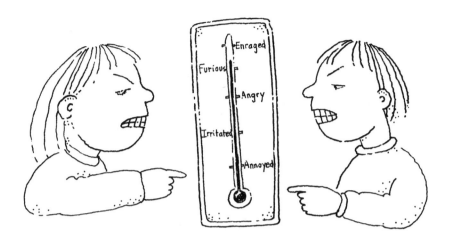

CHAPTER 6

Conflict and Feelings

INTRODUCTION

I was talking with two first-grade girls who were bickering. I was trying to get them to talk things out. Finally one of them said, "I can't talk it out. It feels too bad."

Half of any conflict is emotion, and it is the intense emotions associated with conflict that can make it feel so overwhelming and uncontrollable to children. But children do not have to feel victimized by their own feelings and the feelings of others when they are in conflicts. They can learn to express their feelings without losing control.

This chapter is based on the assumption that anger and other feelings associated with conflict are normal and natural, and that there is nothing wrong with these feelings. These feelings should not, however, be expressed in ways that are destructive or hurtful to others.

Children need the vocabulary to talk about their feelings in conflicts, and they need to be able to identify the triggers that evoke those feelings. They also need to be able to identify the degrees of intensity of feelings, particularly of anger. These skills and understandings take time to develop, and this is an area where it is useful to think in terms of readiness. For most people, learning to handle their feelings in conflicts is a lifelong endeavor.

The activities and books in this chapter focus on the following concepts:

+ *Children should be encouraged to express feelings constructively.*

+ *Children's affective vocabularies can be expanded.*

+ *Children can identify feeling triggers.*

+ *Degrees of anger can be identified using the Anger Thermometer.*

INTRODUCTORY ACTIVITIES

Creating a Feelings Chart

Objectives:

- ✦ *to expand affective vocabulary*
- ✦ *to relate events or triggers to feelings*

Materials:

Large sheet of chart paper

6- by 10-inch cards with the following words written on them:

happy	mad	sad
excited	jealous	angry
lonely	scared	worried
proud	surprised	

SUGGESTED PROCEDURE

1 Display each word card and discuss its meaning with the class. Talk about when the children have felt the feeling written on the card. Then write the word on the chart paper.

2 Have the children pantomime how each feeling looks.

3 Read the following sentences and have volunteers identify the appropriate feeling or feelings for the particular trigger. Add any new feeling words to the feelings chart.

When someone pushes me, I feel _____ .

When I make a mistake, I feel _____ .

When I do a good job, I feel _____ .

When I help someone and they say thanks, I feel _____ .

When someone calls me a name, I feel _____ .

When someone won't share with me, I feel _____ .

When someone will share with me, I feel _____ .

When someone smiles at me, I feel _____ .

When I get a snack I didn't expect, I feel _____ .

Questions for Discussion

- ✦ *Which feeling words do you hear most often?*
- ✦ *Which words were new to you?*
- ✦ *What are some feeling words that are not on the cards?*

Introducing the Anger Thermometer

Objectives:

- *to expand vocabulary of anger-related words*
- *to discuss the differences in intensity of various anger-related words*
- *to introduce children to a metaphor that will help them to control anger*

Materials:

Chart 6–1
Activity Sheet 6-1
Actual thermometer

SUGGESTED PROCEDURE

1 Show a thermometer to the class and ask students to describe what a thermometer does. Ask them to explain what happens to the thermometer when the air gets hotter.

2 Show the Anger Thermometer Chart (or use an overhead transparency made from the chart) and explain that when people get angry, it's as if they get hotter. Their anger can be measured on this Anger Thermometer. Review each term on the Anger Thermometer and discuss its meaning.

3 Discuss how different triggers lead to different degrees of anger by reading the following sentences aloud. As students name their feelings, point to the appropriate word (or words) on the Anger Thermometer.

How would you feel if:

someone took something that belonged to you?

someone kept bothering you while you tried to draw?

someone called you a mean name?

you saw some children teasing a new child in our class?

4 Distribute Activity Sheet 6-1 to each child and have children work in pairs. Each child should complete the sheet individually, and discuss it with his or her partner. With non-readers, continue the above discussion by reading each item on the Activity Sheet aloud and discussing with the class. Discuss the results.

Questions for Discussion

- *What things made you the angriest?*
- *What things didn't bother you very much?*
- *Did you and your partner always feel the same way? How were you different?*
- *What can you do to cool off if you are hot on the Anger Thermometer?*

EXTENSION ACTIVITIES

Ballooning and Draining*

These two activities introduce children to techniques that can help them cool down their angry feelings and come down the Anger Thermometer. *Ballooning* is deep breathing. Have the children stand and tell them to take slow (not deep) breaths and fill themselves up with air as if they were balloons. Then, they slowly let the air out of the balloons. Repeat a few times and have the children explain how they feel.

Draining is consciously tensing and relaxing the muscles in the body. Have the children stand. Ask them to tighten all the muscles in their bodies and hold them tight until you say to let go. After a few seconds, say, "Now relax slowly and let all the anger drain out of you. Imagine a puddle of anger at your feet."

*Adapted with permission from *Creative Conflict Resolution* by William J. Kreidler (Scott Foresman and Co., 1984.)

Feeling Collages

Materials:
    Magazines
    Glue
    Scissors
    Paper

Each child or group of children chooses a feeling word. They write the word on a piece of drawing paper by cutting the appropriate letters out of magazines and gluing them to the paper. Next, have them illustrate the feeling by cutting out and gluing pictures that show faces expressing that feeling.

Feeling Pantomimes

This activity is especially appropriate when you want to do something active. Have the class stand and watch you pantomime a feeling word. Ask them to mimic what you are doing, and then guess what feeling you are miming. After you have done the first feeling, have a student volunteer to come to the front of the room and mime another feeling. The other students first mimic, and then try to guess what it is.

CLASSROOM APPLICATIONS

Day to Day Feelings

One way to encourage children to talk about their feelings is to do it yourself. Start by talking in a matter-of-fact way about your own feelings about various events and activities in the day.

Your goal is to model the use of affective vocabulary and to give children permission to talk about feelings. As you go through the day, ask children how they feel about different events and activities. Encourage them to go beyond, "I feel good about it" and "I like it." Take advantage of opportunities to model use of affective vocabulary. Try to ask about feelings in a way that is natural. You're simply acknowledging that most aspects of daily life have a *feeling* component.

Feelings Check-In

During class meetings, try a *Feelings Check-In*. This can be a simple "go around the circle" with children saying how they feel at that moment. If children need help with words, make suggestions from the Feelings Chart. A variation on this activity is called *Feeling Slots*. Have each student write his or her name on a craft stick or cardboard strip. Collect five or six coffee cans or empty milk cartons. Label each can or carton with a feeling word. At the beginning of the day, have children put their names into the cans that represent how they feel. Repeat after lunch, at the end of the day, and at any other time you choose.

SUGGESTED LITERATURE

Spinky Sulks, by William Steig
New York: Farrar, Straus and Giroux, 1988

Summary

Spinky is angry at everyone in his family, and decides to spend the rest of his life sulking. His family tries to cheer Spinky up, but nothing works until he decides to forgive them.

Before You Read

Tell your students that *Spinky Sulks* is the story of a boy who decides to sulk forever. Discuss sulking and have the children show you what sulking looks like. Ask if they have ever sulked. Why? What are people feeling when they sulk?

After You Read

+ *What were some of the conflicts that led to Spinky feeling so angry?*

+ *Why wouldn't Spinky give in when his family tried to make up with him?*

+ *How would you try to get someone to stop sulking?*

+ *While Spinky sulked, he probably had several feelings. What feelings might he have felt?*

+ *Instead of sulking, how could Spinky have let his family know how he felt?*

FOLLOW-UP TO *SPINKY SULKS*

Sulking Masks

Materials:

Crayons
Paper plates
Scissors
Craft sticks or stiff strips of cardboard

Distribute the materials and have the children draw sulking faces on the paper plates. Help them draw the eyes so that the eyes line up with their own eyes. Then help them cut out the eyes. Staple the masks to the craft sticks or cardboard strips so that children can hold them up in front of their faces. When the masks are complete, choose one child to be Spinky and hold up the sulking mask. Other children play the roles of family members who try to cheer Spinky up.

 *Alexander and the Terrible, Horrible, No Good, Very Bad Day,* by Judith Viorst. New York: Atheneum, 1972

Summary

When Alexander wakes up with gum in his hair, trips on his skateboard, and drops his sweater in the sink, he knows it's going to be a terrible, horrible, no good, very bad day. Alexander's day goes from bad to worse, and he contemplates moving to Australia. Eventually he realizes that some days are bad days, even in Australia.

Before You Read

Have the children brainstorm a list of anger triggers—the things that make them angry. Give the brainstorm about five minutes. When it is complete, review the list with the class and say, "Imagine what it would be like if all these things happened in one day. You'd call that a terrible, horrible, no good, very bad day. This book tells the story of a boy named Alexander, who has such a day."

After You Read

+ *Which of the terrible things were caused by other people, and which were Alexander's own fault?*

+ *How might Alexander have made his day better?*

+ *What words describe how Alexander felt during his no good day?*

FOLLOW-UP TO *ALEXANDER AND THE TERRIBLE, HORRIBLE, NO GOOD, VERY BAD DAY*

How Would You Feel If...

Using Activity Sheet 6-2 and the Feelings Chart created in the introductory activity, discuss how different events can trigger different feelings. Introduce the activity by asking, "How would you feel if someone wouldn't let you play a game? What would that feeling look like?" As children name the feelings they might have, point to the words on the chart. Have the children complete the Activity Sheet by labeling the feelings and drawing faces in the ovals that illustrate the feelings.

My Own Terrible, Horrible, No Good, Very Bad Day

Have students write stories describing what their own terrible, horrible, no good, very bad day would be like. The story should begin when they get up in the morning and continue until bedtime. Encourage the children to illustrate these stories. Make them into books by making covers out of construction paper and stapling the covers and the pages together. Non-readers can dictate stories to you individually or in small groups.

 *The Grouchy Ladybug,* by Eric Carle
New York: HarperCollins, 1977

Summary

An angry ladybug is spoiling for a fight, but can't find anyone who's big enough to fight. After a long day of picking fights, the ladybug arrives home in a very different mood.

Before You Read

Explain that *The Grouchy Ladybug* tells the story of a ladybug in a very bad mood. Discuss the word *grouchy*. Most children will be familiar with the Sesame Street character, Oscar the Grouch. Ask them how people act when they're grouchy. Ask them what makes them grouchy.

After You Read

◆ *Why didn't the ladybug fight the animals? Was it really because they were too small?*

◆ *Have you ever been in a grouchy mood? How did you behave?*

◆ *If the ladybug asked you to fight, what would you say?*

FOLLOW-UP TO *THE GROUCHY LADY BUG*

Animal Weapons*

Materials:

Pictures of animal weapons (horns, teeth, claws, antlers, etc.) or actual objects.

Discuss the animal weapons in the book—pincers, claws, beak, horns, etc. Show the pictures or objects you have collected and discuss how animals use them. For example, claws can be weapons, but they are also used for obtaining food. Conclude the discussion by asking what people can use to solve disputes. Elicit that we have mouths and ears and brains that let us talk out our problems, listen to other people, and think about solutions.

*Adapted with permission from *Creative Conflict Resolution* by William J. Kreidler (Scott Foresman and Co., 1984.)

ADDITIONAL BOOKS ABOUT FEELINGS

Grandpa's Face, by Eloise Greenfield. (New York: Philomel Books, 1988)
Tamika is frightened when she sees how many mean faces her beloved grandfather is making. She doesn't realize that, as an actor, that's his job.

The Little Brute Family, by Russell Hoban. (New York: Macmillan, 1966)
The Brute Family is grouchy and unhappy until the Little Brute brings home a good feeling.

The Teacher from the Black Lagoon, by Mike Thayer. (New York: Scholastic, 1989)
A little boy hears that his new teacher is really a monster, and gives in to his fearful fantasies.

BUILDING ON THE THEME

Feelings Dictionary

Materials:

Five or six sheets of 11- by 17-inch drawing paper
Pencils
Crayons

Label each sheet with a feeling word to be pages in the dictionary. Have children illustrate the feelings dictionary with examples of characters from books who have felt that way. They can write a description of a time a character experienced the feeling, or they can draw a picture illustrating how a character felt during an incident in the story. They also write or dictate the title and author of the book.

Five Feelings Stories

Materials:

Feeling Word Cards from the Introductory Activity

Begin by demonstrating the activity. Draw five word cards at random from the deck of cards. Display the cards and ask, "What kind of story could we create using these five feelings?" With the help of the children, write a short story on the board that incorporates the feeling words you selected. Then divide the children into cooperative groups and have each group draw five cards from their decks of feeling words and create their own stories.

The Anger Thermometer

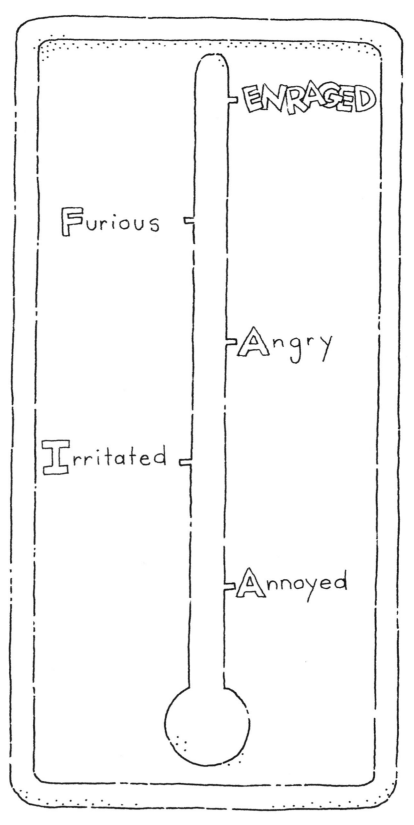

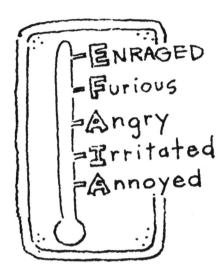

Someone smushes your
snack at snack time.

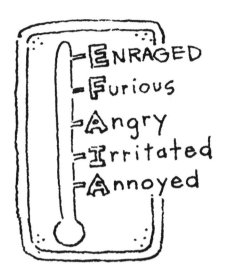

A boy on the bus says,
"You can't sit here. I own this seat."

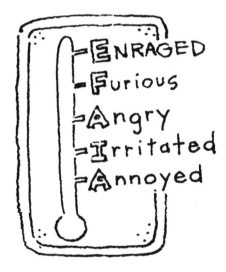

A girl in the hall says,
"You little kids should go
to kindergarten."

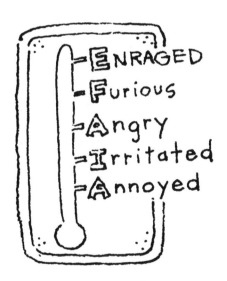

You want to swing,
but the children who are on
the swings won't get off.

WORD BANK: glad sad excited angry lonely scared worried surprised

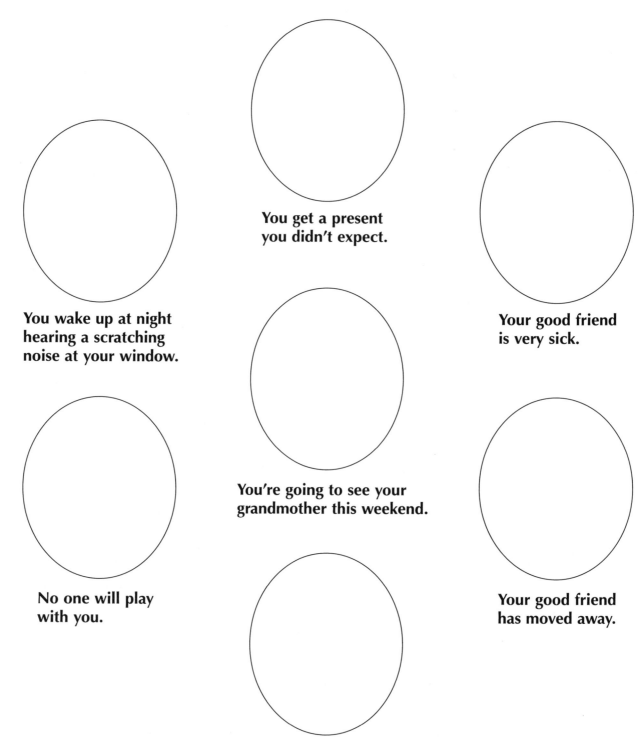

**You get a present
you didn't expect.**

**You wake up at night
hearing a scratching
noise at your window.**

**Your good friend
is very sick.**

**You're going to see your
grandmother this weekend.**

**No one will play
with you.**

**Your good friend
has moved away.**

Someone says, "We want you in our club."

CHAPTER 7

Appreciating Diversity

INTRODUCTION

Several years ago I took my first-grade class to a multicultural fair. As we wandered past the booths of food, crafts, clothing, and saw the variety of people there, I heard one child say to another, "People come in different packages."

Human beings do indeed display a wide and wonderful diversity, a diversity that is the source of much of our growth and progress as people. Unfortunately, this diversity also leads to destructive conflict in a wide variety of forms—stereotyping, prejudice, racism, and discrimination, to name a few. Some of these destructive forms of conflict are present even in young children. Studies show that young children are aware of differences and are likely to judge them negatively based on societal norms. One way to counter the development of prejudice and bias in younger children is to help them see diversity as positive and enriching instead of threatening and potentially harmful.

The activities and books in this chapter focus on the following concepts:

+ *Differences between people exist equally with commonalities.*

+ *Without differences, there would be no growth or progress.*

+ *Without our commonalities, we would have no basis for understanding each other.*

+ *Differences can lead to misunderstandings and conflicts, but these conflicts can be resolved.*

INTRODUCTORY ACTIVITIES

Same and Different

Objectives:

+ *to identify and affirm differences and similarities in classmates*

+ *to encourage children to talk about differences*

Materials:
Drawing paper
Crayons

SUGGESTED PROCEDURE

1 Have children work with partners. Have the partners interview each other to determine three things they have in common (or ways they are alike) and three ways in which they are different. Have them make a list of the similarities and differences.

2 When the list is complete, each child should draw a portrait of his or her partner. Tape or staple the two portraits to the list and display them on a bulletin board.

3 Non-readers can work with their partners to discover one way they are alike and one way they are different.

Questions for Discussion

+ *What were some of the ways you were like your partner?*

+ *How were you different?*

+ *How could your differences lead to conflict?*

+ *What might you do to solve that conflict?*

+ *How might your differences be helpful or useful?*

Pick Your Corner*

Objectives:

+ *to identify how group memberships reflect differences and commonalities*

+ *to discuss how differences can be enriching or can lead to conflict*

SUGGESTED PROCEDURE

1 Designate two corners of the room as *belong to this group* and *don't belong to this group*. Explain to the children that you will be reading statements and you want them to go to the appropriate corner.

2 Have the children stand. Say, "If you belong to the group that likes broccoli, move to this corner of the room. If you don't belong to that group, move to that corner of the room." As you speak, indicate the appropriate corners and have the children move.

Questions for Discussion

✦ *What are some of the good things about belonging to this group?*

✦ *What are some of the disadvantages to not being part of the group?*

✦ *What kind of conflict could occur between these two groups?*

3 Continue the activity with other groups, such as girls, not girls; tall, not tall; bike rider, not bike riders; Latino, not Latino; can tie own shoes, can't tie own shoes; brown eyes, not brown eyes; Catholic, not Catholic; speak more than one language, don't speak more than one language; and so on. The groups you name can be as controversial or non-controversial as you wish, but try to present a mix of choices based on groups formed by choice, interests, personal tastes, ethnic and cultural group, and so on.

Questions for Discussion

✦ *How did you become a member of this group? Were you born into it?*

✦ *Did you choose to be a member?*

✦ *Did you learn something that made you a member?*

✦ *What could you learn from someone in another group?*

✦ *How could different groups have conflicts?*

✦ *How could they resolve those conflicts?*

*Adapted from *Creative Conflict Resolution*, by William J. Kreidler (Scott Foresman and Co., 1984.)

EXTENSION ACTIVITIES

Family Bag Reports

Materials:
> Brown paper bags
> Crayons
> Collected objects

Have the children create *bag reports* that represent their families. On the front of the bag, have them draw pictures of their families. (If the bags have printing, children can draw the pictures on drawing paper and tape the drawing to the front of the bag.) They place various objects inside the bags representing aspects of their family lives. For example, they may collect objects representing:

✦ *something the family likes to do together;*

- *a tradition in the family;*
- *a way a child helps his or her family;*
- *a trip the family took;*
- *a story that the family likes to read.*

Give children a few days to work on their bag reports, and then have them present their bag reports to the class. They should describe the picture on the front of the bag, and then show each object and describe what it represents. As children present their bag reports, discuss how families can be very different but still have many things in common.

Grouping Physical Characteristics

Physical characteristics describe the way people look. Brainstorm with the class a list of physical characteristics and write them on the board. Encourage the children to identify categories of these characteristics. You can use class members to illustrate these categories. For example, children might say that some people have blonde hair, and others have brown hair. Write the category as *hair color*, and encourage the class to identify as many types of hair color as they can.

- *Are people born with physical characteristics or do they acquire them?*
- *Can physical characteristics be changed?*
- *Do all people with the same physical characteristic behave the same way? For example, do all people with brown eyes act the same way?*

CLASSROOM APPLICATIONS

Classroom Inventory

The first step in helping children appreciate diversity is to look at your own classroom and your own behavior. There are simple steps you can take to create a climate that affirms diversity. For example, check the materials in your classroom. When you use pictures for bulletin boards or for discussion starters, make sure they reflect a variety of cultures and skin colors. Include pictures showing disabled people performing everyday tasks.

Review the books in the class library to be sure that they accurately represent different cultures. Check to see if you have books that show women and men performing nontraditional jobs and tasks. Try to include books that depict many kinds of families. You do not need to eliminate books and materials that are more traditional in their depictions of American life, but try to provide a more diverse, more inclusive, and more accurate picture of our society.

Look at the toys, play props, and manipulatives in your room. For example, have you integrated the doll corner with multiracial dolls? Does your housekeeping corner have chopsticks, clay pots, baskets, woks, and so on? Do you include math manipulatives that are rooted in other cultures, such as tangrams and abacuses?

Stereotypes and Misconceptions

When you hear children express stereotypes or misconceptions about different cultures or groups, use these moments to gain insights. Sometimes children make these statements instead of asking questions, and stereotype statements are often a reflection of developmental levels. For example, a light-skinned child may say that dark-skinned children are dirty. He or she may be asking if they *are* dirty. The child may be expressing confusion, rooted in the static thinking of this age group about the permanence of some physical characteristics. Challenge this stereotype by asking children to wash their hands to demonstrate that skin color doesn't wash off.

Modeling an Appreciation for Diversity

Take opportunities to discuss similarities and differences among children. Help them see specific ways that differences benefit the classroom. If children see that you are not afraid of diversity, your attitude will give them permission to talk about differences and encourage appreciation for diversity.

SUGGESTED LITERATURE

Amazing Grace, Mary Hoffman
New York: Dial Books for Young Readers, 1991

Summary
Grace loves to hear stories and act them out. When she learns that her class will be presenting a play about about Peter Pan, she decides that she wants to play Peter. But her classmates say that she can't play the part because she's a girl, and because she's black.

Before You Read
Explain that *Amazing Grace* is the story of a girl who wanted to do something very much that everyone told her she could not do. Discuss the story of *Peter Pan*. If children are completely unfamiliar with the story, read a picture book version.

After You Read

+ *Why did Grace's classmates think she couldn't be Peter Pan?*

+ *What do you think Nana meant when she said, "If Grace put her mind to it, she can do anything she wants?"*

+ *Have you ever had a conflict with someone because you wanted to do something they thought you couldn't do? How did you resolve the conflict?*

FOLLOW-UP TO *AMAZING GRACE*

Different Shoes

Materials:

> Outlines of four pairs of feet

Remind children of how different points of view can lead to conflicts. Place four sets of footprints on the floor. Explain that one set is for Grace, one set is for a boy or girl in her class, one set is for Grace's mother, and the last set is for Nana. Have children stand on each set of footprints to play that character. The other children interview the characters about their respective points of view on Grace playing Peter Pan. Encourage the interviewers to explore why the characters feel the way they do. Demonstrate this activity by asking several interview questions yourself.

 *Frederick,* by Leo Lionni
New York: Alfred A. Knopf, 1967

Summary

The mouse family busily stores food for the winter, but Frederick doesn't seem to be doing any work. "I am collecting colors and stories for the long winter," he tells his family. And when the winter comes, they are indeed grateful for the memories, images, and poems that Frederick shares with them.

Before You Read

Tell your class that *Frederick* is the story of a mouse who is different from the other mice. Have the children sit in a circle. Go around the circle and ask each child to name something that he or she could teach someone else. Are all the things the same?

After You Read

> ✦ *How was Frederick different from the other mice?*
>
> ✦ *How did Frederick's different way help the other mice?*
>
> ✦ *The other mice didn't seem to get angry with Frederick for not doing the kind of work they did. What might have happened in the story if they had gotten angry?*

FOLLOW-UP TO *FREDERICK*

Each One Teach One

Materials:

> Chart paper
> Markers

Make a chart listing each child's name. Next to the names make two columns labeled *I can teach* and *I want to learn*. Show the chart to the class and remind them of the discussion they had prior to reading *Frederick*. Explain that there are many people in the class who have skills to teach. Ask children to think of something they might teach to others in the class and to write that skill in the first column next to their names. There may be some children who need help in thinking of something they can teach to the other students. Children can read the chart and write their names in the second column next to skills they would like to learn.

Chicken Sunday, by Patricia Polacco
New York: Philomel Books, 1992

Summary
Stewart, Winston, and Patricia are friends, and they want to buy Miss Eula an Easter bonnet from Mr. Kadinsky's hat shop. But they don't have enough money. Even worse, Mr. Kadinsky thinks they are the ones who threw eggs at his window. Finally they figure out a way to make peace with Mr. Kadinsky and earn the money they need.

Before You Read
Ask the children if they have ever been accused of something didn't do. How did they explain the truth? In *Chicken Sunday*, children use things from their cultures to solve this kind of conflict.

As You Read
Point out the different cultures that appear in the story. Winston, Stewart, and Miss Eula are African American (Baptist religion). Patricia is a combination of Jewish and Ukranian (Russian Orthodox religion). Mr. Kadinsky is Jewish.

After You Read
- *How did the children resolve their conflict with Mr. Kadinsky?*
- *In what ways were Stewart, Winston, and Patricia like each other?*
- *How were they different from each other? How did this help them?*

FOLLOW-UP TO *CHICKEN SUNDAY*

Peace Eggs

Materials:
Activity Sheet 7-1
Crayons

In *Chicken Sunday*, the children made peace with Mr. Kadinsky by bringing him the pysanky eggs. Discuss the idea of peace offerings that was first introduced in Chapter 3. Ask if they have ever given someone a peace offering. What was it? What happened?

Distribute Activity Sheet 7-1 and have the children draw a picture inside the egg of someone making a peace offering. They may illustrate an incident from their own lives or use a situation from one of the books the class has read.

ADDITIONAL BOOKS ABOUT DIVERSITY

All the Animals Were Angry, by William Wondriska (New York: Holt, 1970)
>All the animals criticize each other because of their differences.

Clive Eats Alligators, by Alison Lester (Boston: Houghton Mifflin, 1986)
>A group of children go through the day, each with unique likes, dislikes, and ways of doing things.

How My Parents Learned to Eat, by Ina Friedman (Boston: Houghton Mifflin, 1984)
>A Japanese woman and an American sailor fall in love and learn about each other's cultures.

Oliver Button Is A Sissy, by Tomi dePaola. (San Diego: Voyager/Harcourt Brace Jovanovich, 1979)
>Oliver Button isn't like the other boys, but they learn to appreciate how his differences enrich their lives.

BUILDING ON THE THEME

Differences Clothesline

Materials:
>Drawing paper
>Crayons
>Yarn
>Spring clothespins

Choose a book you have read to the class to use as a sample. On each side of the paper draw two pictures illustrating two themes. The picture on one side should represent how the characters were different from each other. The second drawing should show how the characters resolved their conflict. Using the clothespins, pin the drawings to the yarn and display. After the children have done or seen a sample, have them choose a book and do a clothesline report.

Chicken Sunday, by Patricia Polacco

Peace Eggs

Draw a picture of someone making a peace offering.

Caring, Respect, and Community

INTRODUCTION

In the introduction to this book, I wrote that my experience shows that children learn conflict resolution best in the context of a caring classroom community. In fact, my experience leads me to believe that they learn *everything* best in the context of a caring classroom community. I believe that when children feel safe, respected, and cared for, they are free to learn. I recently met Denise, a second grader whose teacher worked hard to make a Peaceable Classroom in her inner-city classroom. "I love my class," Denise said. "Those rooms where the kids are always fighting, they're missing out on the real stuff."

Caring, respect, and community in a classroom are not abstract ideals. They are achievable goals, a combination of values, behaviors, and attitudes. They are the "real stuff." The books and activities in this chapter focus on the following concepts.

> ✦ *Specific behaviors encourage community.*
>
> ✦ *Developing the values of helping, caring, respect, and kindness reinforce community.*
>
> ✦ *Children can understand the benefits of being in a caring classroom community.*

INTRODUCTORY ACTIVITIES

Caring T Chart*

Objectives:

- *to identify specific caring behaviors*
- *to reinforce caring as a positive value*

SUGGESTED PROCEDURE

1 Write the word caring on the board. Ask volunteers to define it. Explain that the class will identify ways to make the classroom a more caring place.

2 Make a *T Chart* on the board.

WHAT CARING LOOKS LIKE	WHAT CARING SOUNDS LIKE

Have the children brainstorm specific behaviors for each side of the chart.

Questions for Discussion

- *Why is a caring classroom important?*
- *Which things on our chart could we do right away to have a more caring classroom?*
- *What are good ways to handle conflicts in our caring classroom?*

*"T Charts" are a common cooperative learning activity. I learned about them from Nancy and Ted Graves of the International Association for Cooperation in Education.

Helping Hands*

Objectives:

- *to identify ways children can and do help others*
- *to reinforce helping as a positive thing*

Materials:

Construction paper in red, orange, yellow, green, blue, and purple
Scissors
Pencils

SUGGESTED PROCEDURE

1 Begin by discussing the concept of helping. Ask children how they help other people in school, at home, and in the community.

2 Give each child a piece of construction paper. Have children trace both of their hands and cut out the outlines. On each cutout have children write their names. On each finger, have them write a way in which they help other people.

3 Mount the cutouts on a *Helping Hands* bulletin board. If you have enough hands and colors, try forming the shape of a rainbow.

Questions for Discussion

✦ *What are some of the ways other people have helped you?*

✦ *What does helping have to do with caring?*

✦ *What are some stories where the characters have helped each other?*

*Adapted with permission from *Elementary Perspectives, Teaching Concepts of Peace and Conflict*, by William J. Kreidler (Educators for Social Responsibility, 1991.)

EXTENSION ACTIVITY

Frozen Beanbag

Materials:

One beanbag for each child playing the game

The object of the game is for children to help each other so everyone can keep moving as long as possible. Each player receives a beanbag to balance on his or her head. Each player moves around the room or the designated play area. If the beanbag slips off a child's head, he or she is frozen and must stop moving. Children who see a frozen player should try to help that person by picking up the beanbag and replacing it on the child's head. If the helper's beanbag should fall off, then she or he is frozen as well and needs to wait for help. Soon everyone will be frozen.

CLASSROOM APPLICATIONS

Class Compact

Develop a Class Compact of guidelines for a caring classroom. With young children, use three sentence starters:

In this classroom, we treat people with respect. That means _____.

In this classroom, we care about each other. That means _____.

In this classroom, we use conflict resolution. That means _____.

Present these sentences to the class and focus the discussion on completing the specific behaviors. Try to elicit three specific behaviors for each sentence starter. Write the results of the discussion on a chart.

SUGGESTED LITERATURE

 *A Chair for My Mother,* by Vera Williams
New York: Greenwillow Books/ William Morrow and Co., 1982

Summary
A young girl, her mother, and her grandmother save their money to buy a big, comfortable chair. Finally, they save enough money.

Before You Read
Explain that *A Chair for My Mother* tells the story of a family that works together to save for something. Ask the children if they have ever saved money for something they particularly wanted. Have a few children describe their experiences.

After You Read

   ✦ *How did the neighbors help the family?*

   ✦ *What did the grandmother say about the neighbors? How were they kind?*

   ✦ *What were some of the things the family did in the chair?*

FOLLOW-UP TO *A CHAIR FOR MY MOTHER*

If I Had a Hundred Dollars

Materials:
   Drawing paper
   Crayons

Begin by asking the class to imagine that they had one hundred dollars to give away. They may give it to any person, group, or organization. Ask a few volunteers to explain their ideas. Divide the children into cooperative groups of three or four and distribute the materials. In the center of the paper, have the children draw a $100 bill. Then each child in the group draws a picture to show how he or she would spend the money. The children should label their pictures, saying who receives the money and why. A variation on this activity is to have the children make the decision as a group.

 ## *Teammates,* by Peter Golenbock
New York: Harcourt Brace Jovanovich, 1990

Summary
Jackie Robinson was the first African-American Major League baseball player. As a result, he faced discrimination and conflict wherever the team went. This book tells the story of his courage.

Before You Read
Explain that *Teammates* tells of how two friends helped each other to be brave. Discuss discrimination—treating people unfairly because of the way they look or because of choices they make. Explain that for many years African-American people were discriminated against in some parts of the United States. Ask if the children know of any examples of discrimination.

As You Read
Point out the examples of discrimination that are described in the book.

After You Read

+ *How did Pee Wee Reese show that he cared about Jackie Robinson?*

+ *Why was it dangerous for Pee Wee Reese to show that he cared for and respected Jackie Robinson?*

+ *How do you know that Jackie Robinson was a brave man?*

+ *How do you know that Pee Wee Reese was a brave man?*

FOLLOW-UP TO *TEAMMATES*

Silent Caring

Materials:
Activity Sheet 8-1
Crayons

When Pee Wee Reese put his arm around Jackie Robinson, he was telling the crowd, "I am standing by him. This man is my teammate." Pee Wee Reese did not use words, but everyone who saw his action knew what he meant. Using Activity Sheet 8-1, have pairs of children act out each of the caring statements nonverbally. You may wish to begin by reading the statements together.

Mufaro's Beautiful Daughter, by John Steptoe
New York: Lothrop, Lee and Shepard, 1987

Summary

Mufaro has two daughters. Nyasha is kind and considerate, but Manyara is selfish and bad-tempered. When the king decides to take a wife, Manyara decides that she must be chosen.

Before You Read

Ask the children how people in their families show that they care for each other. After volunteers have responded, explain that *Mufaro's Beautiful Daughter* tells of a girl who showed many people and animals that she cared about them.

After You Read

+ *If Nyoka the snake was going to give advice to Manyara, what do you think he'd say?*

+ *Nyasha was rewarded for her caring behavior. What good things have happened to you when you've showed other people that you cared?*

+ *In what ways are you like Nyasha? In what ways are you like Manyara?*

FOLLOW-UP TO *MUFARO'S BEAUTIFUL DAUGHTER*

Nyasha's Way

Materials:

Activity Sheet 8-2

Crayons

Drawing paper

Have children work in pairs. Distribute Activity Sheet 8-2 and have the children decide how they think Nyasha would respond in each situation. Have them complete each sentence and draw a picture on a seperate piece if paper illustrating her response. They can cut out and glue their sentences to the pictures. For non-readers, use the Activity Sheet as a springboard for discussion.

ADDITIONAL BOOKS ABOUT CARING

She Come Bringing Me That Little Baby Girl, by Eloise Greenfield. (New York: Harper-Collins, 1974)

Kevin is disappointed and jealous when a new baby sister arrives in the house. But gradually he learns to love and care for her.

Two Good Friends, by Judy Delton. (New York: Crown Publishers, 1974)

Rabbit and Bear are friends, despite the fact that Rabbit is neat and Bear is messy. Each finds a way to show care for the other.

Ty's One Man Band, by Mildred Pitts Walter. (New York: Scholastic, 1980)

Ty is has nothing to do while everyone is working hard. Andro, a circus performer, teaches Ty how to make music on ordinary objects, and he shares this gift with everyone in the neighborhood.

BUILDING ON THE THEME

Caring T Chart for Books

Repeat the Introductory Activity, *Caring T Chart*, but have children cite specific caring behaviors from books. Make a T Chart on large paper and post it in the room. Each time a specific caring behavior is recorded, also record the title of the book and its author.

WHAT CARING LOOKS LIKE	WHAT CARING SOUNDS LIKE
Nyasha gave the old woman water. (*Mufaro's Beautiful Daughter* by John Steptoe)	Grandma said, "You are wonderful people." (*A Chair for My Mother* by Vera Williams)

Saying "I Care" Without Saying a Word

Draw a picture to show how you would show each of these statements:

Glad to meet you.	You're my friend.
I'm glad you're here.	Don't feel bad.
Hooray for you!	You did a good job.

**If Nyasha saw children
arguing about the rules of a game,
she would . . .**

**If Nyasha saw her sister
blaming her brother for letting the yams burn,
she would . . .**

**If Nyasha saw two brothers
telling a younger brother he couldn't play with them,
she would . . .**

**If Nyasha saw a bully
who was taking sunflower seeds from other children,
she would . . .**

About the Author

William J. Kreidler is a former elementary teacher with over twenty years of experience. He is an internationally known expert in conflict resolution and violence prevention. He is the author of the popular guides for teachers, *Creative Resolution* and *Elementary Perspectives: Teaching Concepts of Peace and Conflict,* and the newly published, *Conflict Resolution in the Middle School.* His column, "The Caring Classroom," appears monthly in *Instructor* magazine. He has been associated with Educators for Social Responsibility since it was founded in 1982.

Mr. Kreidler is a popular speaker and workshop leader, and he has worked with teachers and students all over the world on issues of conflict resolution, violence prevention, appreciating diversity, and of course, children's literature. He is currently working on a companion volume to this book, *Teaching Conflict Resolution Through Children's Literature, Grades 3-6,* to be published by Scholastic. Mr. Kreidler can be contacted c/o The Peaceable Classroom, P.O. Box 391553, Cambridge, MA 02139.

Boston Area Educators for Social Responsibility is a chapter of the national organization of Educators for Social Responsibility. Boston Area ESR, located at 19 Garden Street, Cambridge, MA, 02138, offers programs for school systems and teachers in a number of areas, including conflict resolution, violence prevention, environmental education, and children's literature to name a few. Each year Boston Area ESR presents an award to a children's book author who promotes such themes of social responsibility as caring, conflict resolution, appreciation for diversity, community, and cooperative problem solving in his or her work.

Notes

Notes